SEX APPEAL OF THI

Sex Appeal of the Inorganic

MARIO PERNIOLA

Translated by
MASSIMO VERDICCHIO

NEW YORK • LONDON

CONTINUUM
The Tower Building, 11 York Road, London SE1 7NX
15 East 26th Street, New York, NY 10010

www.continuumbooks.com

This English translation first published in 2004
English translation © Continuum 2004

First published in Italian as *Il sex appeal dell'inorganico*
© 2000 Giulio Einaudi s.p.a. Torino

Massimo Verdicchio has asserted his right under the Copyright, Design and
Patents Act 1988, to be identified as the author of this work

British Library Cataloguing-in-Publication Data
A catalogue record for this book is available from the British Library.

ISBN 0-8264-6244-8 (HB)   0-8264-6245-6 (PB)

Typeset by Aarontype Limited, Easton, Bristol.
Printed and bound in Great Britain by Antony Rowe, Chippenham, Wiltshire

Contents

1

Senses and Things

To give oneself as a thing that feels and to take a thing that feels is the new experience that asserts itself on contemporary feeling, a radical and extreme experience that has its cornerstone in the encounter between philosophy and sexuality, and constitutes the key to understanding so many disparate manifestations of present-day culture and art. What may generate anxiety and constitute an enigma is precisely the coming together of two opposite dimensions in a single phenomenon such as the mode of being of the thing and human sensibility. It would seem that things and senses are no longer in conflict with one another but have struck an alliance thanks to which the most detached abstraction and the most unrestrained excitement are almost inseparable and are often indistinguishable. Thus, out of the union between philosophy's speculative extremism and sexuality's invincible power something extraordinary is born in which our age recognizes itself, and which after Walter Benjamin we can call the sex appeal of the inorganic.[1]

2

Sex Plateaux

The alliance between the senses and things allows access to a neuter sexuality that entails a suspension of feeling. This is not the annulment of sensibility, which would imply the absence of any tension, but the entrance into a displaced, decentred experience, freed of any intention of reaching a purpose. To feel like a thing that feels means first of all the emancipation from an instrumental conception of sexual excitement that naturally considers it directed toward the attainment of orgasm. The usual way of representing sexual activity by means of a diagram that measures excitement precludes the mode of being of the thing. As long as we think of sexuality in terms of a curve that, starting from zero, rises more or less slowly toward the acme of orgasm, only to decrease suddenly and return to the starting point, we remain a victim of an attitude that experiences sexual feeling as a more or less long preparation for a very brief climax destined to precipitate to the zero point of a normality deprived of tension, from which it seems that one has never moved after all. To devote all one's attention to the prolongation of the preliminaries of sexual intercourse and to attribute to orgasm a cathartic and liberating meaning precludes from the start the possibility of feeling like a thing. Thus, one is stuck within a model that compares sexual feeling to mountain climbing which, on the one hand, implies a slow and progressive climb, and, on the other, a precipice whence one must necessarily throw oneself to return downhill in ten seconds. The relation between sexuality and knowledge has so far been left obscure and inscrutable because a valley mentality has prevailed which has separated with the greatest precision a normality without tension from the exceptional nature of sexual ascent and descent. After all, how can a speculative attitude originate in a process that is made up of a merely instrumental and preliminary first part and a very short second part that cancels hastily what was prepared with so much care? It is hard to avoid the impression that something one wants quickly to return to zero cannot, indeed, be worth more than zero. To free oneself of orgasmomania, which has raged for decades and has conditioned negatively the lives of generations, is the first step toward the neuter, suspended and artificial sexuality of the thing that feels. It emancipates sexuality from nature and entrusts it to artifice, which opens up a world where the difference between the sexes, form, appearance, beauty, age and race no longer matter.

3

God, Animal, Thing

Having exhausted the great historical task of comparing man to God and to the animal, which in the West began with the Greeks, what claims our attention now and raises the most urgent questions is the thing. It has become the focus of both our preoccupation and the promise of happiness. The play of resemblances and differences, affinities and divergences, correspondences and disparities that has characterized the comparison between God and man, and between man and animal, has concluded in a tie. Man is an almost God and an almost animal. God and the animal are almost man. But who has the courage or the desperation to say that man is an almost thing and the thing an almost man?

Upon the vertical movement, rising toward the divine or descending toward the animal, follows a horizontal movement toward the thing. It is neither above nor under us, but beside us, to one side, around us. The high and the low, the lofty and the depths have ceased to constitute the reference points that give meaning to the life of the individual and the community. On the other hand, ecstasy and instinctual liberation, rapture and vital effusion, do not seem to be so opposed as tradition has made them out to be. To become God or animal, to rise spiritually or to behave like a beast, are they so different from each other, after all? Are they not both animated by an excitement, an agitation that can be defined as either spiritual or vital, divine or animal? One thing is sure. In both the divine and the animal throbs and beats the living, while this is not the case with the thing which we encounter as both the anti-divine and the anti-animal, as what makes it possible to grasp the complementarity that holds God and animal together.

The comparison requires, therefore, a more radical alterity than the divine and the bestial. Up to now the issue has been resolved in a very expeditious and casual manner by stating that the animate being feels while the inanimate does not. Feeling, then, marks the boundary between the living and the thing. Therefore, how can one say that man is a thing that feels? This definition appears absurd at first because it is not enough to add feeling to the mode of being of the thing to come up with man. But who is looking for man? Rather, it's a question of finding the thing. Maybe the thing is a man who does not feel? Or who feels a little?

If I say that the thing is a man that does not feel, I place man once again at the centre of the universe and I make him the measure of the world. In this anthropologization of inert beings, a deep transformation of the human occurs that makes him completely alien and unrecognizable. Is it enough, then, that the paper on which I write perceives the movement of the pen on the page in order to seem already human? Is it enough that the pen feels the pressure of my fingers in order to erase all differences between it and myself? How is it possible that the great and infinite life-world has been erased to such an extent? How is it possible that all my humanity is only concentrated in the feeling of a pen that presses on me or of a hand that holds me tight? How is it possible that nothing else matters and has value outside of this contact where all experience and knowledge, all that one has loved, suffered, sought and known, is gathered and concentrated? How is it possible that the entire order and balance of life rotates around a pressing or a squeezing? Is it possible that everything is already given in this feeling as pen and paper? What promises and oaths, tears and embraces, may not add to the feeling of a thing that feels?

In fact, this is the great transformation that we are witnessing and of which we are the protagonists, that is, no longer to feel like God, or like an animal, but as a sentient thing for whom the least perceivable is the maximum perceivable or, better, in the least perceivable there is the maximum perceivable. In such drastically sensitive reductionism, we capture not the being in itself of the thing, its essence, or what it would be without the presence of man, rather, a human feeling reduced to its lowest terms. However, this minimum feeling does not seem to lose anything. In the slightest contact there is implicit all the superhuman and the infrahuman of which we are capable, all the hopes and abjections, all the intellectual and practical world. It is ready to spurt out from that point in which it is forced, limited, compressed and ready to unfold in a great wealth of man-ifestations, developing an operational effectiveness that extends to any field of activity. Therefore, when I say that man is a thing that feels, at first I extinguish, blunt and close off the feeling, or, at least, I take away its liveliness, its brio, its flagrancy, but secondly I promote its extreme sharpness, I make it similar to a point, to a needle, to a sword.

4

Descartes and the Thing that Feels

A thing that feels seems somewhat different from a thing that thinks and moves. These last two notions are not a novelty as they have already been the object of Descartes's meditations. The thing that thinks is the mind for which the self-consciousness of the I, and the idea of God as a very perfect being, is essential. The thing that moves is the machine, whose model serves to explain the functioning of living bodies, men as much as animals. The mind and the machine are the two things that make it possible to establish, on the one hand, a comparison between man and God, and, on the other, between man and animal. It sounds strange, however, that they are called 'things'. In fact, the mind is a spiritual substance clearly distinct from the body and, therefore, at first sight, it is extraneous to the dimension of the thing. As far as the body is concerned, even though qualified by extension, it presents, essentially, dynamic characteristics that make it more similar to a functioning mechanism than to an inert thing. In fact, no lesser action is required for its rest than for its motion. Nonetheless, Descartes calls them both 'things' and considers the I to be a thing that not only thinks but also feels because of the fact that it is connected to the body. Feeling implies the union between body and spirit, mind and machine. A thinking thing can also not have a body, but a sentient thing has to have it. Who feels therefore is not God but the I, it feels because it thinks, because feeling, understood in its self-evident subjectivity, is none other than thinking.

On this self-consciousness, Descartes founds his entire house of knowledge. Although, in his view, the thinking thing exhausts itself in the subjectivity that is aware of its existence, both the thing and the feeling constitute a remainder that is not absorbed in the clarity and distinction of self-evident thinking. If I say that man is a thing that feels, the being thing of what it feels and the feeling of the thing require a greater recognition than Descartes was prepared to grant them. The thing and the feeling demand to be considered in themselves and not in the function of a thinking subject. The strangeness of this request depends on their union. They have made common cause against the Cartesian thinking I who understands the thing as subject and feeling as thinking. According to Descartes, the thinking thing has superiority with respect to all the others because by virtue of its thinking it discovers that it exists, while to other things is not permitted the self-evidence of one's own existence. In so doing, however, he considers the notion of thing as synonymous with substance and foundation, in a metaphysical sense that completely disregards the neutral dimension which is implicit in the notion of thing. As far as feeling is concerned, according to Descartes, it is not separable from thinking and from willing. The union of these faculties constitutes, precisely, a subjectivity that thinks itself as thinking, but not as an entity for which knowledge and action are rather a consequence of feeling.

What if feeling was not necessary to the subject? did not suit a subjectivity that says 'I'? What if it were not able to grasp feeling as such unless it were on condition of transforming it into thinking? What if feeling were not accessible to an I? What if any effort made by the I to appropriate feeling were to lead inevitably to thinking? What if in feeling there was implicit and essential a neutral dimension that compelled us to say: 'one feels', but prevented us from saying: 'I feel'? What if any attempt at saying: 'I feel' were to fatally resolve in 'I think'?

The history of the modern appropriation of feeling by thinking begins precisely with Descartes for whom the thing that feels with immediacy and evidence is not the body but the mind. According to Descartes, from my body, from the extended thing that belongs to me, no clear and distinct knowledge can reach me directly. It is not any more evident to me than external bodies. However, this does not mean that my body is separated from the mind, but only that the mind feels what occurs in it. One would be tempted to claim against Descartes the rights of the body, considering it the bearer of a stronger and more vivid sensitive evidence than the intellectual one. But this is the way of sensationalism that in reducing all knowledge to a sensation has always been the poor parent of Cartesian rationalism.

The problem we have before us today does not concern the origins of knowledge, whether it is reflection or sensation, mind or body. At this level Descartes's victory is definitive, only the mind is a thing that thinks, not the body. Not even opposing the thought of the mind to a supposed autonomous feeling of the body takes us very far. If feeling is thought of as something subjective, both in the first instance and in the last instance it can be referred to the self-consciousness of the mind. The rock on which Cartesianism trips is not the ignorance of the body, or its relation to it, but the very idea of a thing that feels.

Anyway, is the thing for Descartes really only metaphysical substance? He also speaks of the most common, inanimate, inert thing, for instance a piece of wax. If we remove all that does not belong to the wax, says Descartes, such as its colour, figure, size, what is left is 'something extended, flexible, and changeable',[2] capable of taking on an infinity of shapes. Since the shapes that the wax can take are numberless, none of them, according to Descartes, is reliable. My senses do not allow me to see what the wax is, it is my mind alone that, after 'the clothes have been taken off it', succeeds in seeing it entirely 'nude' (II, 14). This is what interests us and this is what today we are comparing it with, not the thing that thinks, or the one that moves, and not even the thing that shines in a certain, stable sensitive form, but something opaque, indeterminate and open which is not self-evident and is not a machine. Maybe it feels? But what does it feel?

However, to say that the thing is 'nude' is misleading because it means that once more the demands of knowledge prevail over those of feeling; it means expressing a prejudicial suspicion on what is external. It means pretending to find the naked truth under deceitful appearances. From the point of view of feeling, the thing is rather clothing than nudity. It is similar to those 'hats' and those 'clothes' under which, for Descartes, 'automata might be concealed' (II, 13). Here, however, we must leave Descartes to his ghosts and his machines. We would like to bring our attention to those hats and clothing.

5

Becoming Extraneous Clothing

The body experienced by neutral sexuality is not a machine, but clothing, a thing. It is made of many types of fabrics juxtaposed and interwoven among themselves. To give oneself as a thing that feels means asking that the clothes that make up the body of the partner are mixed with one's own, thus creating a single extension in which one can travel for hours, for days. To take a thing that feels means asking that one's own clothing be welcomed everywhere and for always, to the point of no longer being recognized either by oneself or by one's partner as belonging to someone. Thus the difference between giving and taking disappears and an extraneous body or, better, extraneous clothing appears that does not belong to anyone. Bodies have become rolls of material that fold and unfold on one another, so that, finally, it is possible to establish a new order, laying silk with silk, wool with wool, cloth with cloth. The tongue that permeates me and covers me, the sex that penetrates me and wears me, the mouth that sucks me and undresses me, all are clothing metaphors. The organs are clothes whose buttons and seams have vanished and return in the condition of pieces of material ready to be worked on. Thus, they can be united and separated according to new criteria that do not correspond to any function or purpose.

It is not I, it is not you that feels, but those hats and clothes mentioned by Descartes. They begin to feel from the moment in which they lose their shape of hats and cloaks, returning to be felts and fabrics that offer each other to one another, and that accept one another, without the intervention of spirits or machinery. Often I ask myself where this clothing libido comes from that cannot be satiated because it is not a hunger. It is pure and radical as the experience of philosophy, which with an incredible determination has always pretended to reduce to a few principles and concepts the immense variety of the world. Instead of the swarming and turbid viscosity of life, neuter sexuality opens up the timeless horizon of the thing. It is as if the bodies removed from the confused and contradictory vicissitudes of life were given the serene and eternal simplicity of an inorganic world, which nonetheless feels, beats and is caught in endless astonishment.

The cold lens of philosophy dismisses the tumultuous ambiguousness of the soul that constantly jumps here and there and is crowded and bewildered by opposite and incompatible representations. The fleshy clothes of our bodies are just like those that we leave on the armchair at night before we go to bed. Finally they are removed from the enantiodromia of contrary sentiments, the perennial chasing after each other of love and hate, attraction and repulsion, tenderness and aggressiveness, and the turning of one into the other. The folds of the female sex are no different from the depressions of a seat cover, the skin that runs along the rod of the male sex is similar to the covering of an arm rest. The fleshy clothing of our bodies, liberated from time and suspended in an enchantment without expectation, are the object of an infinite and absolute sexual investment that would seem more appropriate to a tailor, a seamstress, an upholsterer gone mad than to a philosopher. And yet, today, it is precisely up to the philosopher to proclaim the greatness and dignity of a sexuality without life and without soul. It is his task and his responsibility to state that the kingdom of things is not so much the triumph of technology and capitalism as much as the empire of a sexuality without orgasm. Thus, finally, it is precisely within the sphere that seems most irrational, casual and fragile, that of sexual excitement, that the power of philosophy is demonstrated, to whose appeal I am incapable of resisting, even if I wanted to.

Philosophy's extraordinary power of excitement is probably connected to the fact that it has a similar power of inhibition. As long as sexuality is tied to vitalistic and spiritualistic representations, the sharp feeling of philosophical abstraction functions as a block; thus, and not without irony, one could recommend a philosophy course to those who suffer from premature ejaculation. Students of philosophy who have been lucky enough to have had a good teacher know very well that his mental image has an inhibitory effectiveness, beyond compare, greater than any other. But even this obstacle has its positive side because it teaches us to be detached from any orgastic vitalism and from any spiritualistic superelevation that marked the cultural experience of sexuality of the first part of the twentieth century. It seems that the moment has finally come to dismiss D. H. Lawrence and Henry Miller who were the harmful spokesmen of the former, as well as Julius Evola whose mystical sexuality inspired by the Orient exercised a profound underground influence. Paradoxically, one gets closer to neutral sexuality by abstinence, than by means of vitalistic and spiritualistic experiences that pass animal exuberance or the superelevation of the soul for sexuality. The dissoluteness of the former and the elevation of the latter lead now to ridiculous, now to tragic situations, but in any case they are far away from the impression of a limit-experience that accompanies the offering of one's own body as extraneous clothing not to pleasure or to someone else's desire, but to an impersonal and insatiable speculative excitement that never tires of traversing it, penetrating it, wearing it, and that enters, insinuates, sticks into us, opening us toward a complete exteriority in which everything is surface, skin, fabric.

This offer, however, is not something merely passive, is not something that one suffers, something to which one submits out of complaisance or curiosity. Anyway, it can occur since, in its turn, it already takes the body of the partner as thing, participates in an intellectual, emotional and sensitive horizon without subject, shares a fever for roaming, for excess, for radicality; it has decided with courage and purity to go forward in the adventure of philosophy. In fact, a lot of purity, honesty and even candour, are necessary to become clothing. In fact in this process there is no longer room for the crafty individual who plots his own advancement, who makes plans and dreams up intrigues, who hides in the caves of his secret intentions. There is not even room for the person who has renounced his own will in order no longer to be in disagreement with the real, who has annulled himself to approve unconditionally what happens, who has become a nobody in order to be always victorious.

In neutral sexuality, philosophical and sexual excess nourish one another. Philosophical adventure seems tasteless and tarnished if it does not entail at least the possibility of transiting to a real dimension, in the etymological sense of the word *res* (thing) and, vice versa, the sexual adventure remains trivial and spiritless if it is not followed by a determination to pursue extreme consequences, which belong to philosophical thinking. This marriage of philosophy and sexuality, which in the experience of the West has always been implicit and virtual, unfolds today with explosive intrusiveness because both the one and the other succeed in absorbing in themselves what still resisted them as opposite and inaccessible, namely, the mode of being of the inorganic, the not living and not functioning.

The philosopher who feels that he is a thing has the impression of transgressing the tradition that represented him as a subject, person, spectator, actor. But at the same time this transgression is a loyalty to pursue that movement of paradoxical innovation, overcoming and surpassing required both by Hegel and Nietzsche. The lover who gives himself as thing has the impression of subverting a tradition that saw him as living, desiring, pleasure-loving, moved now by animal now by spiritual drives. At the same time this subversion allows him to include the neuter in sexuality, completing that movement of libidinal appropriation of the opposites that led Sade and Masoch to sexualize fear and pain. It is as if philosophy and sexuality found in each other what was necessary to accomplish their own historical journey. In the experience of becoming extraneous clothing meets the speculative suspension of libido and the sex appeal of philosophy.

6

Exemplary Addictions

If we look in our common experience for something that may be analogous to the neutral feeling of becoming thing, we find it in drug addiction and, in particular, those addictions caused by opium and its by-products. From De Quincey to Burroughs an entire literary production describes the splendours and miseries of drugs. What is striking is the opposition between the addictive experience and the sexual organ, as well as the importance given to the world of things in perception. The general tonality of the drug addict seems characterized by feeling one's own body as thing, by making the body extraneous like clothing, by removing oneself from the cycle of tension, unloading and rest. This literature has emphasized the connection between the depersonalization and the suspension of subjectivity caused, on the one hand, by the use of drugs and, on the other, the development of the poetic spirit. It is connected to the elaboration of a theory that considers the poetic process as the advent of an impersonal and autonomous word, more similar to a thing than to a mood or to a manifestation of a will. This way, it has anticipated contemporary sensibility in which feeling exhibits the traits of the greatest artificiality.

However, in the actual assertion of the experience of drug addiction as model and paradigm of any feeling, the poetic adventure finds its own crowning as well as its own overcoming. In fact, the thing we are confronted with is not just a poem or a work of art. The thing that feels is really man. Paradoxically, philosophy, from always being the friend of virtue, seems to reach it more easily than poetry, which has always been surrounded by a halo of recklessness and transgression. The entrance of philosophy into the world of excess is more essential and disturbing than that accomplished by poetry and literature. In fact, it is not a question of getting inspiration from immoderate and excessive experiences in order to compose texts or write books, but of understanding philosophy as a practice that creates a dependency similar to that instituted by drugs, as a need that cannot be satisfied unless in a temporary and unstable manner, because it is infinite. After all, starting from the moment in which the mode of feeling of addiction moves from the pathology to the physiology of contemporary society, how can intellectual activity, of which philosophy is the example par excellence, and bodily activity, of which sexuality is the example par excellence, maintain themselves and survive unless by supporting one another and by originating a new experience? Now, it is true that philosophy has very often been considered with suspicion, and sometimes it has been criminalized and condemned, as in the case of Socrates and Bruno, but, notwithstanding this millenarian struggle for survival, it has never lost the hope of constituting a guide for private and collective life. Similarly, it is true that for two millennia we have seen in sexuality the most common and frequent sins, but precisely for this reason it was the object par excellence of repentance, forgiveness and absolution. Precisely because of its oscillation between loving sublimation and animal degradation, it seems deserving of leniency, because in both cases it generated a benign disease culminating in the redeeming and cathartic moment of orgasm.

The scene opened by drug addiction is much more gloomy and dark because it does not compare with the divine or with the animal world, which, in the last instance, are both reassuring, because almost human, but with the inanimate and opaque world of things, from which is precluded any possibility of redemption. The union of philosophy and sexuality in the neutral experience of giving oneself as thing that feels, creates a state similar to that created by drugs, because one is heedless of everything that is not one's own infinite continuation and repetition. Neutral sexuality sets up an infinite dependency because it is removed from biological rhythms and cycles. It is constituted by the radical movement of philosophy and is nourished by its excessive and uncompromising thrust. It is not at all a question of using common drugs as instruments for philosophizing or for the practice of sexuality – to have interesting thoughts or some exciting images – rather, that the encounter of philosophy and sexuality generates a similar effect as opium and its by-products. Thus it seems that philosophy and sexuality move on the side of evil in a much more essential and constitutive manner than ever before. Evil here is not spiritual evil symbolized by rebellion and by diabolical challenge, or the bestial type of orgies and debauchery, but the inorganic evil of dependency and being unable to do without something physical, just like the substances used by drug addicts.

When you find the realization of the Cartesian thing that feels in the cunnilingus or in the fellatio of your partner, when you notice in the coherent and rigorous unfolding of philosophic prose the inexorable movement that brings you to lick the cunt, the cock or the arse of your partner who has become a neutral and limitless extension of cloth variously folded, when you yourself are able to offer your body as a desert or a heath so that it can be traversed by the detached and inexorable examination of the eye, the hands and the mouth of your lover, when nothing else interests you or excites you or attracts you besides repeating every night the ritual of the double metamorphosis of philosophy into sex and sex into philosophy, then, maybe, you have both moved onto the side of evil and vice, you have celebrated the triumph of the thing over everything, you have led the mind and the body to the extreme regions of the non-living, where, perhaps, they were always already directed.

Maybe this is the only way left that they may still experience. From this statement, one can deduce two completely different orders of considerations. In the first place, we can say that since the experience of drug addiction has become the model of every radical and extreme feeling, philosophy and sexuality are equally obliged to adapt to its modalities. The becoming extraneous of the morphine addict's body would have acquired in our time an exemplary dimension such that everything that aspires to some emotional and sensitive importance resembles it, just as in the past all intoxications were similar to those caused by wine. Or one could say that neutral sexuality to which philosophy leads us constitutes the point of arrival of a journey that has always already belonged to it. Thus the impression of inexorable and desperate dependency that becoming a thing that feels generates is only hesitation, fear, resistance in the face of a new scenario whose protagonist is not God, or the animal and not even man, but the thing. To be sure, it is strange that the union between philosophy and sexuality occurs under the sign of drugs and not under that of wine, but this seems to be a necessity imposed by having to appropriate a sphere not yet explored, both philosophical and sexual. The philosophical *sobria ebrietas*, sober intoxication, does not lead us toward the thing. From Socrates to Nietzsche we know everything on the relation between wine and philosophy. In it sexuality has played without doubt an important role, but not an essential one, because it has always flowed up or down, absorbed by spirit or life. Neutral sexuality, instead, does not flow. All the metaphors derived from ejaculation and the flow of menstrual blood must be abandoned. This does not mean that the thing is stationary. The thing transits, does not flow. Even in its movement, in its changes, it preserves its opacity, its non-spiritual and non-vital, non-mental and non-functioning character. It seems a vice precisely because it does not flow away, because it is always there, always given, boundlessly available, open, without redemption and without satisfaction, without catharsis. It seems a vice because it is not a means to reaching some external purpose, noble or ignoble as it may be, because it breaks up constantly the course of time and dislocates the machine, introduces us into a movement without time and without purpose, sufficient unto itself, which asks only for its continuation.

7

Kant and the Spouse as Thing

And what if the mutual and reciprocal give and take as things were not a vice at all but a virtue, in fact, the only moral condition in the exercise of sexuality? What if to entrust the unconditioned possession of ourselves to someone who gives himself or herself with equal and unconditioned compliance constituted not the extreme experience of evil, but, on the contrary, the very essence of marriage understood as the only state that allows a rational and lawful practice of sex? Although it may appear surprising at first, this is Kant's thesis, according to which man cannot make use of his body as he wishes because he does not have possession over it, it does not belong to him, he is not the owner of his sexual faculties. Who is the legitimate owner of my sexual organs? According to Kant, I am not, but he or she who makes me the owner of his or hers. My freedom, autonomy and independence find their own limitations in sexuality, or, better, they can only be exercised negatively in abstention and renunciation, and not positively in renting me out, as in prostitution, or in giving me to someone who does not give himself, in his/her turn, in an equally unconditioned way as in concubinage. The essence of sexuality is not located in a *vague libido* that the subject controls and runs as he wishes, it is not something subjective. When two subjects, says Kant, satisfy reciprocally their *vague libido*, without any other interest beside the service that each renders the other, it would seem that there is nothing unbecoming. But is this sexuality? Is not sexuality rather the movement in which I give myself infinitely to someone who in his/her turn gives him/herself to me in the same way? How can we arrive at the neutral and boundless heath where the master finally takes possession of what always already belonged to him and will always belong to him at the moment when he recognizes and offers himself and always as slave? But this can only occur in wedlock which 'is based on the right to dispose of the person in his/her totality'.[3] In fact, says Kant, 'this right to dispose of someone else's person is in regard of the entire condition of his happiness and any other circumstance that concerns him'. In wedlock each entrusts his/her entire person to the other in order to acquire full rights on the whole person of the other.

It is very significant that Kant who is the philosopher of subjectivity par excellence would see in sexuality something that leads 'to the highest form of reciprocal submission between two people'. Unlike so many beautiful souls who believe that the freedom of the subject can get along with sexuality, Kant is not deceived on this score. He realizes very well that in the 'appetite' of having the other as thing, which one can treat as one pleases, there is inherent 'a principle of degradation of human nature'. From the point of view of subjectivity, in the very sexual act 'resides something despicable and contrary to morality'. To be sure, to consider the other as thing that feels seems somehow like an insult, but this humiliation can be overcome only by a similar giving oneself to him as thing that feels, reconstituting thus a unity of wills in the common determination of traversing the infinite spaces opened up by becoming thing. Those who pretend to reduce sexuality to need, friendship or a recreational relationship make the same mistake as those who believe that philosophy is a good sense activity, a practice of average virtues or a sensible exercise. In actuality, there is in sexuality as in philosophy an excess which is essential to them, which constitute them as such, which is disrespectful of one's own and other's liberty, that makes them similar to the slavery and dependency of drugs. Precisely because of their excess, sexuality runs towards marriage and philosophy toward the university. If they were reasonable and liberal, as the beautiful people of sexual liberation and university protests pretend, they would never shut themselves in the prison of marriage and philosophical schools. It is time to see marriage and the university on the side of evil, as pushers of sexual and philosophical excess that one cannot do without, rather than on the side of good as remedy to sexual and cognitive libido.

In Kant's theories of the relation between sexuality and marriage, however, it is easy to detect an uncertainty, an unresolved problem. Kant fully recognizes the reifying character of sexuality, its compulsion to give and take absolute power. Therefore, he is extraneous to the ideology of adelphic and comradely marriage of pietistic memory, and unites sexuality and marriage inseparably. But if marriage implies reciprocal reliance of one's entire person on the other and thus encloses within oneself that mutual devotion which is the secret spring of sexuality, how can it be defined as only a contract? In Kant's legal definition, isn't there something too restrictive and limiting, too tied to the independence and the autonomy of the subjects, too conditioned and too desexualized? Here the theory of faculties and the alienated sexual parts of the spouse come into conflict with the fundamental formulation of Kant's philosophy. How can I give to someone by means of a contract something that I do not own, as Kant says? Those who consider marriage a sacrament, don't they see deeper into the essence of sexuality? Those who consider it as pertaining to *fas*, divine right, rather than to *ius*, human right, don't they have a better grasp of the nature of marriage?

8

Sadism and Sex Appeal of the Inorganic

It would be wrong, however, to consider neutral sexuality as a reciprocal master and slave relationship, where the partners offer themselves to one another in turn in absolute and unconditional submission. To be sure, in order to access the anonymous and impersonal territory of things that feel, one must be able to say 'do with me what you wish' and be transported by an irresistible excitement in assisting the transformation of the person who burns and throbs in your arms to an inert and opaque entity which, nonetheless, is so receptive and sensitive to feeling the most tenuous caress, the most imperceptible kiss, the slightest touch. To be sure, one must use the greatest cruelty in delaying the least perceptions, the transits, the modulations, the variations of feeling, so as not to give too many stimuli all at once, in too many places, at the same time. Certainly one has to be able to see that absence, silence, abstention are no less harsh and bitter than the unlimited exercise of arranging, ordering, demanding any services, subduing, squeezing and traversing the boundless regions of the body, ruling over them as if they were the clothing in one's wardrobe, the pillows of one's couch, the carpet of one's floor.

But the impersonal dimension into which neutral sexuality introduces us has little to do with a master and slave relationship. It does not introduce a relation of equality in sadism since it lacks the premise of sadism, the appointment of a strong, autonomous, independent subject, master of himself who asserts himself and triumphs in a practice of appalling negation and destruction. After all it is absurd to think that a sadist could acknowledge to someone other than himself the right to display and express the infinite energy that animates him. And if he is prepared, at any moment, to change his role of executioner to that of victim, it is not because he agrees to a recognition of reciprocity, to the possibility of taking turns, but because even in misfortune and in defeat he is ready to assert his own happy and victorious uniqueness. The art of constant enjoyment, of finding one's own exultation in any state and condition, of discerning infinite occasions of voluptuousness even in torment, torture and death, is an ability that the sadist can only acknowledge to himself and no one else because it does not stand on an abstract principle but on the challenge that he has made to God and His creation at the moment when, in renouncing forever the possibility of constituting with others a unity of wills, he has bet everything on himself and on the unlimited reinforcement of his sovereignty.

The sex appeal of the inorganic also originates from a challenge, an intimation that first of all one experiences oneself, from a gathering of faculties in a single decisive point on which everything depends. But even though he asks and urges his partner to give herself without reservation, it does not accumulate and build up in the formation and consolidation of a subject understood as a substitute of God. It is not I who command you to take me in this or that part of the body, to offer to me this or that caress, to give yourself in total submission, but it is the world of things that demands it. We can access it only if you make me feel that your body is completely available to everything that an impersonal feeling prescribes.

Sometimes, it seems as if even in sadism there is at work an anonymous energy, a destructive and annihilating force of which the libertine would be the simple carrier, but it is, after all, only a type of vitalism in reverse that finds its fullness in a single will which is posited as absolute and unconditional. When we enter the horizon of neutral sexuality, instead, there is no particular will, but only the experience of an impersonal saying, of a voice that speaks both for you and for me. The idea of the individual as entity surrounded by a halo of inviolable intangibility may have its own legitimacy at the political level, but at the level of sexuality it leads to a frigid and bloodless comradeship that wears out and exhausts itself in a chain of permission, consent, concession, almost as if every embrace were the result of a more or less explicit negotiation, of timid and embarrassed requests, of awkward and uncertain favours. To introduce politics into sexuality, as was the case in the past, entails a greater violation of decency than that perpetrated by those who err in calculating equalities, because by not knowing the exact measure of give and take, they exceed in asking; because this excess can be remedied by the infinite reversibility of the master and slave relationship, while a lack of generosity, an initial meanness, a prejudicial pettiness bar access to the accessory experience of neutral sexuality.

The English language, which makes use of the second person plural pronoun 'you' for any type of relation, is at first sight the least suitable to allow the passage from relations of negotiations between autonomous and independent individuals to relations of sexual dependency. However intimate was the relation that I had with an 'English-speaking' partner, I always had the impression that I never succeeded in going beyond the limits of a business transaction whose object is the exchange or the acquisition of sexual favours. Perhaps one should try and erase the capital 'I' and use 'you' even for oneself, thus becoming estranged from one's own body. With the frequency that the practice of flagellation appears in the erotic literature and iconography of the eighteenth and nineteenth centuries, it is perhaps possible to find a corrective and an overcoming of the permanent negotiation inherent in language. In fact, even though to flagellate and be flagellated were for the most part paid services, in any case they introduce into the logic of interest a contradiction that undermines and dislocates the linguistic–sexual order. What is certain is that the neutral sexuality of the things that feel is incompatible with the reification of sex. Prostitution, generally, gives too little to be able to arouse neutral excitement. The thing that feels is not a commodity. Even if in the idea of prostitution seems implicit the dissolution of subjectivity, this always reappears in commercial transaction whether directly or indirectly.

If anything, the thing that feels is closer to money which combines in itself the characters of anonymity and availability. But the relation of greatest dependency cannot come from an alterity that calls us and that we call with the pronoun 'you'. It can be flagellated and flagellate as much as it wants. Only the second person singular 'thou', used in prayers, can open the door to neutral sexuality. This prayer goes like this: *thou* do with me what you wish!

The relationship that sadism entertains with politics is not any less complex than what it has with economics. Reversing a tendency that considers sadism at the service of politics, Pasolini in his film *Salò. The hundred and twenty days of Sodom* places politics at the service of sadism. In it, four brutal libertines take the opportunity offered them by the absolute power of Fascism to retire to a castle with twenty young men and women to subject them to all sorts of humiliation, torment and torture. Pasolini wants to underscore, in this fashion, the relation that links sadism to power, but he does not succeed in showing that it is essentially political. The fact that many who have pursued and achieved absolute power were in fact motivated by more or less sadistic intentions, is a suggestive idea that would make it possible to read the entire history of mankind *sub specie libidinis*. But the privilege of sharing a mutual relation with sexuality is the right of philosophy alone, whose power is neither sadistic nor bloodthirsty. Philosophy alone, in fact, has the capacity of reaching that extreme excess that Pasolini pursues with obstinacy in his film. The sadistic search occurs under the sign of frustration and defeat. One can burn breasts and testicles, pull teeth and eyes, impale, skin and flay to infinity without succeeding in reaching that excess that philosophy achieves with chastity.

Nagima Oshima in his *Empire of the Senses* (*Ai no korrida*) has gone further in exploring impersonal and anonymous energy. The film narrates the irresistible unfolding of sexual will pursued to the castration and death of the loved one. Here sadism is practised on a partner who collaborates and is agreeable, who does not shirk from the demands of an absolute and total power, and who makes his own in the most radical way the assumption that his lover initially proposed to him: 'Do with me what you wish.' In fact, the person who pronounces this sentence has thrown a challenge to his own partner that sounds something like this: 'Are you capable too of offering yourself to me in the same way?' – so that this proposition can also be a trap that a sadistic mind can prepare for his generous lover. But next to this noble emulation to become an inert and infinitely sentient thing in the hands of whoever takes you, next to this contest in sacrifice and immolating oneself to the triumph of a sadistic energy, next to approving and executing what is demanded of you until the union with a repulsive body, until the acceptance of pain and death, there is in Oshima's film an experience of life as malaise, as discomfort that can be mitigated only by becoming the object of attention of a sadistic sexuality both tireless and irrevocable. Starting from the moment when the sadist takes on the appearance of the nurse, the nun, the assistant who assuage the hurt and the pain of living, we enter in the deepest and most disquieting dimension of the sadistic world. In fact, he does not become the dispenser of positive pain, and not even of positive enjoyment, but of relief, a pharmakon that does not heal, but gives relief, alleviates, tempers the infinite agony of existence. Thus, if life is suffering, having found someone prepared to cut off your penis while he chokes you to death is great happiness. Your torture is a good death and the sadist a benefactor. Perhaps the time has come to remove euthanasia from the depressing and demoralizing view of a minor evil, to place it within the sphere of sadistic sexuality. Unfortunately, only those who in life were already ready to die for you can bestow on you the good death, or, better, only those who in life have given their body, without reservations, to a sexual energy of which you alone were the vehicle. Too often, instead, one unites one's destiny and spends one's whole life with someone with whom one has not even for a moment gone beyond the logic of negotiation and pseudo-egalitarian comradeship. But with what could you ever negotiate your good death if not with the one you were asked to give? But those who say: 'Do with me what you wish' are already extraneous to any past, present or future negotiation.

The empire of the senses, that is the infinite search for always new sexual sensations, proves the inability of sexuality to reach excess on its own. Even though the experiences to which this search leads are unusual and extreme, they always contain elements of disappointment and dissatisfaction, almost as if sexuality, left in its purity and not sustained by anything else, contained a tendency to self-annihilation and self-destruction in orgasm and death. There is no doubt that sadism practised on a consenting subject is qualitatively different from criminal sadism, even though both are very distant from the neutral sexuality of the thing that feels. If criminal sadism is the extreme affirmation of the individual subject, consenting sadism is the seal of the pact of alliance that creates the collective subject. It is nice to be able to say 'us' instead of 'I' in the exuberant wealth of feeling-together that runs toward death. Very often, it seems to us that the future could not have a better end in store for us than being accompanied in the extreme hour of death, especially if it is made in the permanence and invariance of a sexual offer. However, the experience of this death is still and always the continuation of vital frustration, is the mitigation of a suffering without truce which is intimately connected with living. Not even if my sacrifice is the execution of the prayer 'Do with me what you wish' am I capable of reaching an excess that could really mark a turning point with respect to an always dissatisfied and disillusioned temporal subjectivity.

Philosophy alone makes this turning point possible because it interrupts and suspends the rush toward the surplus and the different and introduces us to the neutral and impersonal experience of the thing that feels, by removing sexuality from vitalism and sadism. The excess of philosophical sexuality is not something that one reaches through a progressive increase of sensations and situations but is already given all at once. It is born from the transformation of the subject into sentient thing. This experience does not need a surplus because it is already greatly transgressive and excessive because of the radical negation of the individual and collective subject that it implies. It neither states: 'I feel' nor 'we feel', but asserts impersonally 'one feels'. It does not require an always new and greater profanation, a violation that goes beyond the previous ones, because it is already completely outside the horizon of the divine. It does not replace God with the I because the place of either one or the other is already taken by the thing. Similarly it does not feel that life is pain alleviated by the exercise of sex and, perhaps, eliminated with a common death, because things know neither life nor death, and are not even prisoner of a subjective and self-conscious subjectivity that closes them in themselves and from which they feel the need to escape at any cost.

The transgression of neutral sexuality is already entirely in a shared and self-evident knowledge. Not only is the tongue that licks in cunnilingus or in fellatio the same that can explain Kant, not only is the excitement that keeps it going a continuation of the excitement felt in reading Kant's works, but this sexual activity is intimately and essentially connected to a critical reflection, to a speculative consideration of Kant's philosophy, and not a philological one. The moment I say 'Do with me what you wish', I feel that Kant could never have said it, but that I can say it thanks to him alone, and not to Sade. This is because Kant is the bearer of a greater radicality, because my invitation has meaning only on condition of seeing it as the point of arrival of a journey in which he occupies a central place, because the unconditional way in which I can give myself and ask that others give themselves is somehow legitimated and authorized by the categorical way in which, in his view, moral law asserts itself on the subject. In fact, if the tendency to take a thing that feels and to give oneself as a thing that feels depended only on subjective cupidity or intentionality, it would be too mobile, uncertain and capricious, as in the case of Sade's libertine. In order that something can excite infinitely and unconditionally, it must come from something equally infinite and unconditional. At the empirical level not even death can be the guarantor of an experience of excess. Sexuality becomes the ally of philosophy in order to find the way out of the dead end to which sadism leads it not only as the criminal will of the individual subject but also as the suicidal will of the collective subject. The things that feel do not need to unite in a death project to be certain they are together.

9

Philosophical Cybersex

The transformation of the subject into a thing that feels seems part of an imaginary science fiction world where the organic and inorganic, the anthropological and technological, the natural and artificial overlap and blend in one another. In fact, from the moment when science fiction introduced intermediary figures between man and robot that share aspects of both, a new problematic opened up that refers to the nature of a feeling which is not yet fully human (as in the case of the replicant, the android and the simulacrum), or which is no longer human (as in the case of the cyborg, that is of a man into whose body numerous prostheses have been introduced). Nevertheless, the general orientation of this imaginary figure remains more or less humanistic and naturalistic. Even though these intermediary forms are sometimes superior to man in the specific functional services for which they have been produced, from a global point of view they remain inferior to their inventor and creator. This dependency on the human model characterizes not only the replicant, whose difference with respect to the original, although not visible, remains relevant, but also the cyborg that cannot be anything else but a developed and perfected man.

Neutral sexuality opens up a dimension that does not constitute an actual anthropological mutation but suspends man, so to speak, in a different virtuality both from what is given and from imagination. The body which is in my arms is as true as mine, but they cease to be obvious to one another, because of their absolute mutual willingness. If both were to run toward orgasm, they would be immersed in that temporal and historical normality that would expose them to perishableness and corruptibility. The cyborg of science fiction escapes them through the substitution of organs with artificial devices. For instance, instead of eyes it has cameras, instead of ears antennae, or the whole body is replaced by a box or a uniform. But these changes are too functional with respect to human needs to generate excitement. To be sure, somehow they are things that feel, they are input with information connected to a power plant that alerts them, but they lack that artificiality without purpose and without limits which is typical of philosophical thinking and neutral sexuality.

Replicants and cyborgs, in general, are too dependent on naturalistic data. Now, reality is not anything empirical but the product of a special effect that creates wonder, requires attention, and asserts itself with surprising actuality. In Ridley Scott's *Blade Runner* a replicant rebels against his condition and pretends to have an autonomous emotional and sexual life. This claim generates in the viewer great expectation as to what would be the sexual feeling of an artificial being. But this expectation is bound to lead to disappointment because the character in question aspires only to a supposed human normality. On the other hand, one cannot even consider as reference points for a neutral sexuality the other figures of science fiction like the alien, the mutant or the unmentionable and unrepresentable thing. Neutral sexuality is not inhumane or inhuman, it is, perhaps, posthuman in the sense that it finds its starting point in man, in his drive toward the artificial that constituted him as such by separating him from the animal, in his will to make the greatest virtuality coincide with the greatest actuality (as in money), in his irreducible tendency toward an excessive experience. It radicalizes something that is already there, preserving it, conserving it, giving it a stability without compare and greater than the natural given. The latter, in fact, is essentially precarious.

Neutral sexuality can be considered a virtual sexuality, a *cybersex*, but not in the commonly understood sense of an illusory experience of sexuality which, thanks to technology (headsets, gloves, suits) is lived as real. This interpretation of virtuality is too dependent on a would-be sexual normality. We begin to enter into the problematic of virtual sexuality only from the moment in which we ask ourselves how it is possible to stir up sexual excitement at any moment and to maintain it for an indeterminate time avoiding the naturalistic cycle of desire–orgasm–relaxation. Virtuality is not simulation, imitation, mimesis of reality, but the access, so to speak, to another ontologically different dimension.

When we speak of virtual realities, we usually emphasize the chimerical and immaterial character of these experiences. This premise is shared by both the apologists of the new virtual technology, who celebrate it as a dissolution, a lightening or spiritualization of reality, and by the critics who interpret it as one more deceit, an evasion that helps us escape the weight, the responsibilities and dangers of the present, by projecting us in an evanescent and disembodied world. Both of them take for granted that virtual realities are not true realities but at best systems of representations of reality that aspire to take its place. This ambition is seen by the apologists as a type of liberation from the anguish and narrowness of reality, and by the critics as a type of guilty escape from it. But reality is not something obvious and stationary! Virtuality does not increase but reduces the level of precariousness of the real. It allows man to move from the era of representation to that of availability. Virtual things are constantly at our disposal. All is offered and this offer constitutes, precisely, its virtuality.

Therefore, a virtual sexuality is not precarious or ephemeral as is the natural one, but is always available in its dizzy artificiality. One can access it through philosophy which creates the condItions of a constant excitement. The sexual–philosophical cyborg, in fact, is always able to be excited and excite. How can philosophy achieve such extraordinary results and become a reliable aphrodisiac? As long as man remains an almost animal or an almost god we are stuck within orgasmic functionalism and ecstasy. The philosophical–sexual cyborg, instead, is an almost thing. Its sexuality depends on the ability to feel the body as thing, but this capacity is accessible through philosophy, precisely because it is able to evaluate fully and in its purity the transgressive force of this idea.

There are at least two philosophical ways of feeling the body as thing. The first perceives the single organs separated from the unity of the body. In this type of experience a single part of the body of our partner becomes the object of extreme attention, of sexual investment that severs it from the living and functioning organism. We perceive the organ as somewhat independent, endowed with autonomous sensibility. It seems at first a little animal that stretches, shrinks, inflates, expands, enlarges. If we stop at this initial impression, we don't go further than the idea of the body as a plurality of animals, or vegetables, each without ties to the other. We sink our hands, our mouth, our tongue in the vagina as in the mouth of a dog, we suck the penis as a snake, or the anus as a flower of flesh. In so doing, however, we do not move far from biological naturalism which in the end blossoms and dies in a relaxing and soothing orgasm. We are left within the sphere of the precariousness of nature and the succession of birth and death. Our sexuality is not capable of being emancipated from the edifying and recreational horizon in which it has always been immersed. We have not yet accessed the artificial and always available world of things that feel.

This access is made easier if we start from parts of the human body that are less sexually characterized or that present a less organic and less sensorially receptive dimension as, for instance, the knees, the breath, the hair. When you caress the knees of your partner you can also imagine that they are not bones but metallic or plastic joints. As for breath, in this context it does not evoke life as breath, but the idea of an immaterial movement qualitatively very determined that comes from inaccessible places. The breath unites the greatest sensorial stimulation, because it strongly arouses our sense of smell, with the greatest abstraction, because it evokes two cavities, the lungs and the stomach, which we will never be able to penetrate. We smell very well their epithelial covering or their content, but they cannot be reached and remain abstract, however much one pushes one's penis into one's partner's mouth. Sometimes, in this act are combined the nobility and beauty of the eyes that stare at us, with the baseness and poverty of sucking, just as in the breath, the noble exhalation of the lungs, which one imagines having a pinker and thinner coating than the vulva's or the anus's, mingles with the heavy exhalation of the stomach's contents, to which could be added, alas in an invisible way, our own sperm. In the conjunction of two aspects of different and uncomparable nature, which however have deep resonances in our feeling, resides the guarantee of an excitement that we can activate at any moment. For instance, the corneous quality of hair gives an impression of the inorganic. But hair, at the same time, presses with force to come out of the cutis of the head, so that the absence of life of the thing is connected with the experience of an abstract power. More generally, this first modality of feeling the body as thing is not without links to a desexualization of the sexual organs, and, reciprocally, to a sexualization of other organs. These as much as the others, freed from a relation of functional dependency with respect to the rest of the body, seem to become capable of an autonomous sensibility of which the subject knows nothing. The sexuality of the organ without body derives precisely from the fact of perceiving it as a sensitive prosthesis, an artificial device endowed with an independent perception entirely its own.

The second modality of the philosophical–sexual cyborg is the body without organs. In this case one arrives at a neutral and impersonal feeling through the defunctionalization not just of an organ, or many organs, but of the whole body, which is no longer perceived as a machine but an extension that nothing separates from the body of one's partner. The impression that the body is no longer useful for anything is connected to the notion that life is no longer worth living, unless it is the unlimited continuation of this state in which all needs and all desires are suppressed. In fact, we cannot even speak of continuation because everything seems stationary in its being given in the co-presence and co-existence in a boundless state. The body without organs is the equator of the flesh, the point when it reaches the everlasting fixity of things. In truth, we are dealing with things that have no figure or that are more extended than we expect, such as the bed sheets of a triple bed, or a deserted beach, or the sea without waves or noontime wind. The body without organs is a field of flesh which is illuminated by days that have the same duration as nights, which is submerged in a climate without variations. It is a territory that does not know seasons, which is always collapsed in humid sultriness that decomposes and undoes all forms. The body without organs, which does not belong to one's will, does not obey any project, and is free of any ties, seems to melt in a fluid that has nothing vital or spiritual. Here the formless liquid is not a metaphor for the mobility of the living soul. One cannot escape the experience of the thing that feels. Therefore, the body without organs is not even an experience, but rather an experiment that succeeds only when any subjective experience has become impossible. It is not my body that takes off in ecstasy or yours. It is not even correct to represent the body without organs as the result of the union of two bodies whose materiality is undone in an infinitely consuming and rending embrace. The body without organs is after all always a cyborg, not a gelatinous blob that overflows from the bed and pours all over the floor. The connections and penetrations do not occur between my body and another's but between a body which is as little mine as it is little the other's. Although I give myself to my partner, she succeeds in taking only my organs as long as she feels this taking as a subjective appropriation of myself. Body without organs means that between my body and hers there is no difference, because both are one thing that feels, a thing to whom we lend, so to speak, our sensitive apparatus so that it may feel. It is precisely this neutral feeling of a body that does not belong to anyone, but whose sensitivity we can always access, that makes it into something always available, so as to arouse infinite excitement. It is there, always ready and wide open in all its extension. Its virtuality depends on the fact that we have the possibility of accessing a coitus between bodies that do not really belong to us. We experiment a coitus, so to speak, which is almost extraneous to our body lived as an organic entity. But one cannot even say that the body without organs is an animated and anthropomorphized thing because it has no real autonomy with respect to us. The body without organs acts sexually, unfolds, develops and multiplies its carnal works, only on condition that we lend it our feeling. It is this lending, precisely, the fact that you do not give yourself to me but to an anonymous and impersonal cyborg which we both enter, that detaches us from the need of running toward orgasm. The moment when we enter the neutral sexuality of the body without organs everything has already occurred.

Therefore, I do not take you, and least of all your cunt, your mouth or your anus but a body, a body that is already the whole of our bodies united. If, then, I picture it to myself as a computerized image, or as the table on which I take you, or as the floor on which our bones are in pain, all this is irrelevant. The essential is that it is not I, not you, but is the philosophical–sexual thing, the maximum abstraction and the maximum reification, that celebrates its triumph over all the projecting subjects and all the utilizable objects, over the world of expectation and instrumentality, over the reign of banality and the obvious.

The organs without body and the body without organs are not the only two modalities of the philosophical–sexual cyborg. There is a third one that originates from a simulated sensorial deprivation. Lie down in a state of absolute rest with your eyes closed as if you were dead. You are deaf, mute and blind and you remain like this despite any appeal, incitement or solicitation. Of all the senses only the sense of touch is left but you cannot exercise it actively. All your attention is concentrated on what brushes against you, touches you, feels you and only on the basis of this pressure are you able to picture the form and the shape of the hands that touch you and caress you, that penetrate into the folds and into the cavities of your flesh. You have never seen, or heard anything, or know the meaning of the silent question of what plods panting over you. Also, all reaction or reflex is precluded to you. You must not give any sign of life, or laugh if you are tickled, or utter moans, cries, or react minimally to any stimulation that becomes progressively more intrusive, that persists in provoking a reaction, that does not withdraw but attacks those parts that they imagine are the most sensitive. This faked death, however, is without frigidity. Your abandonment does not exclude: on the contrary, it implies that whoever devotes himself to you will move your legs, open your mouth, lift your head as he wishes.

At the same time you are not in a state of complete imperturbability, total insensitivity, but, on the contrary, you will concentrate in trying to gather the greatest possible amount of information through touch, the only sensorial door still left open to you, in order to compensate for the enormous disability with an equally enormous concentration on what was given to you. Whoever acts on you, whoever applies the greatest possible effort in exciting you with their hands, mouth, tongue, their sex, in more parts and simultaneously, will get the impression that your body is traversed by an extreme tension that cannot be expressed in any way. In fact, any participation, intervention or adherence is precluded to you. You are a sentient thing that does not favour any act, does not facilitate any penetration, but is there spread out to receive with zeal all that the partner will be able to offer. And when he inserts his penis in your mouth that he will have opened with his hands, he will ask himself how strange must feel the penetration of an almost finger on which the skin slides. While in the organ without body, artificial sexuality is constituted by the prosthetic effect and in the body without organs it is provoked by the displaced extension of the senses, in this third modality, it arises from the simulation of a lack. It seems that only by starting from a handicap may it be possible to reach a surplus of excitement, almost as if the simultaneous attraction of all five senses bewilders in vain, creates psychic confusion and prevents sensorial concentration. The scientific imagination points to the possibility of an intrusive sensor that by bypassing the mediation of the organs and linking the computer directly to the brain, provides the sensorially handicapped with a virtual experience of seeing and listening. What constitutes a cyborg, however, is more the development and intensification of a single sense than the virtual exercise of the others. The door to the sense of touch opens to excess only if the doors to the other senses are temporarily shut.

These three modalities of sexual artificiality, the organs without body, the body without organs and the compensating disability cannot be practised by themselves, they are not forms of masturbation. They require an interaction, a feedback between intelligent and sensitive partners. It is difficult to enter neutral sexuality alone, even with the help of a machine. The philo-sophical–sexual cyborg exhibits an intrinsic sociality that does not depend on inter-subjectivity but on a relation of inter-face that passes not between two subjects but between two almost things. Precisely from this reification depends the permanent actuality and availability of excitement. If it were natural, spiritual or historical, its effectiveness would be temporal and ephemeral. On the other hand, this artificiality is not something mechanical as a conditioned reflex. The sentient prosthesis, the equator of the flesh or the perceptive disability always provoke excitement for cultural and philosophical reasons connected with the experience of being a thing that feels, with the alienation inherent in such practices, with the libido of giving oneself and taking boundlessly.

10

Kant and the Feeling of the Thing in itself

In the idea of the man as thing that feels seems implicit a complete suppression of his dignity, of the respect that he owes to himself and to others in as much as it is a being who has an end in itself and that, therefore, must not be used as means. For Kant, in fact, respect refers only to people and not to things. The assimilation of the human being to a thing, and the persistence in underlining the sexual specificity of a reification that reveals itself to be greater than any form of prostitution and slavery seems inspired by a depravity and a perversity that go well beyond the simple abandonment to sensitive inclination, and that, therefore, were described by Kant as manifestations of a radical evil.

And yet Kant himself is the author of a reflection on the notion of thing in itself and on the relation that it entertains with morality, from which it is possible to draw conclusions that are completely different from those mentioned above about the philosophical meaning of the relation between man and thing. The starting point of Kant's reflection is the distinction between the thing in itself and the thing with respect to us, that is, the phenomenon. Only of the latter is knowledge possible because it is mediated by the subjective forms of intuition (space and time) and by the categories of the intellect. The thing in itself or noumenon, detached from any relation and set in its unconditional absoluteness, has no determinate content. It is objectivity understood in its most complete abstraction.

As long as we limit ourselves to thinking of the thing in itself from the point of view of the theory of knowledge, it is a limit-concept that by definition remains extraneous to human experience. On the one hand there is the thing in its unattainable distance, on the other there is man as subject, self-awareness, synthetic and relational activity. Between the two no meeting point would seem possible and the moral problem should be posed on the side of subjectivity and phenomenon. Instead, just the contrary of what we would expect is the case. With a daring move, of which we are only aware today, Kant bases his moral doctrine on man considered as being in itself, as noumenon. The fundamental law of pure practical reason, which dictates that one should operate in such a way that one's maximum will can always count in every epoch as the principle of a universal legislation is, according to Kant, a fact of reason, an unconditional given that cannot be deduced from previous elements. Nonetheless, the absoluteness of being in itself has a limitation. Man can also will the opposite of the law, he can be moved by sentiments that are connected to subjectivity. If the will could not escape the moral imperative, man would be a saint.

What is striking about Kant's morality is the impersonal, neutral, categorical character of the moral imperative, and the absolute lack of respect with regard to pleasure and pain, desire and fear, and the most complete indifference with regard to success or accidents. This mode of being does not belong to man as animal or man as God, but to man as thing in itself, who, however, has a motive: he is moved by an autonomous feeling completely independent of the subjective affections and which, in fact, is essentially opposed to self-love and presumption. What does the thing in itself feel? Respect, the only rational senti-ment which is at the same time submission to an order and emancipation from desire. It implies humiliation of the subject and elevation of the will that feels it.

The thing in itself, therefore, has nothing to do with the object, the instrument, the means. In fact, it is precisely the opposite. The noumenal, and not phenomenal, character of moral life enjoins one to operate in such a way as to treat humanity, in one's own as in the other's person, always as an end, never as a means. To be a thing in itself is not a mode of degrading or humiliating humanity, but of freeing it from the anguish of the empirical world, from the chain of needs and desires. The moral feeling, such as Kant describes it, shows a close affinity to the neutral and anonymous feeling of a sexuality without orgasm. In both cases, one is freed from the chain of causality, without entering into the oversensitive world of sanctity or ecstasy. The thought that morality and sexuality are in a relation of analogy generates an excitement in which it becomes impossible to distinguish the philosophical from the physical aspect, to the point that one does not know whether the former ought to be thought of as sublimation of the latter, or if the second constitutes the development of the first. What unites them, in fact, is the complete submission to a neutral entity which now is present as duty and now appears as sex appeal of the inorganic. One as much as the other is moved by a drive toward radicality and excess, with regard to which life with all its pleasantness and variety no longer has any value. But what is surprising and astonishing is the enigmatic ambiguity of the notions of freedom and respect both in moral and sexual feeling. In the former, independence with respect to the phenomenal world is conquered at the price of total submission to the categorical imperative. In the latter, autonomy with respect to instrumental intentions consists of unconditional obedience to neutral and impersonal drives that lead to the experience of one's own body as thing. In the former, humiliation and debasement of all subjective claims are accompanied by an edification deriving from the effective action of the moral law on themselves. In the latter, the irreverent and shameless exercise of one's own and the other's body is connected to a sentiment of delicate veneration, sweet concern, consuming devotion with respect to things destined to deteriorate, become corrupt and disappear.

Between moral law and neutral sexuality there is however a difference that confirms, paradoxically, their reciprocal belonging together. Kant's thing in itself is also a thing in itself, a thing by itself, isolated and closed in itself which, to be sure, becomes for itself, that is self-conscious, but from which is precluded the happiness of transiting, moving toward something that can also be reached by others. Nonetheless the refusal to consider happiness as the determining motive of moral life places Kant at the opposite end of selfishness. Thus, it seems that that very powerful drive toward the being thing (neither subject nor object) that animates his morality is interrupted and blocked by the identification between the person and the thing in itself. It is sexuality that allows us to place the thing beyond the person, to make us thing. For Kant, instead, the person, in so far as it is a rational being, is already a thing in itself, a noumenon. Although he postulates in the human being a tendency toward evil, thus making morality more lively and dynamic, this movement rests entirely in the thing in itself. It is not difficult to notice a contradiction between externalization, the alienation implicit in being thing, on the one hand, and the folding back on itself inherent in the notion of personality. Therefore, Kantian morality is susceptible of two developments: one toward the interior, the spirituality of the person, the other toward the exterior, the thingness of sex.

11

Masochism and Sex Appeal of the Inorganic

If sadism opens a horizon of excess, masochism establishes a series of limitations that restrain the claims of the subject and vouch for him in the face of defeats. The masochistic relation is instituted on a free understanding, an agreement, a contract in which the person that proposes it and formulates it undertakes to give himself as slave to a partner, which in the novels of Leopold von Sacher-Masoch is always a woman, who in exchange is obliged to be the actor of sexual scenes and ceremonials entailing the humiliation of the subject. The typical example of this behaviour is that of a woman who is wearing a fur over her naked body who whips a man who is subdued and submissive. What masochism and neutral sexuality have in common is the will to give oneself absolutely as a thing that feels, the irresistible drive to establish a relation in which it is always possible to arouse and maintain sexual excitement. The motto *semel verum, semper verum* (once true, always true) applies equally to both. Both want to tie the partner to something lasting and stable through paradoxical procedures and devices.

Masochistic thinking originates from a very simple question. How can one have the guarantee that an extraordinarily satisfying sexual relation can repeat itself ad infinitum with equal satisfaction? Good sense replies negatively to this question, placing it in the ambit of illusions, dreams and utopias. The demand for perpetuity inherent in the sexual give and take runs against an immovable scepticism. The incredulity about the indefinite duration of sexual attraction is based, to be sure, on orgasmomania and on orgasmolatry of animalistic vitalism, but, more profoundly, it is anchored in the general resignation and acknowledgement of the mutability and precariousness of all earthly things. An eternal love already seems within the order of the impossible, let alone an unlimited sexual excitement. The masochist starts off precisely from this obviousness which, however, he finds unacceptable. Therefore, it seems to him that the best way to overcome the liability of pleasure and its inconstancy is to view it as already finite. His strategy consists in placing himself not before but after the disaster. He plays beforehand and does not wait for the sexual passion of his partner to diminish little by little and to look for new objects of attraction, turning to indifference and hostility. He does not wait to come into conflict with the loved one, but he already declares himself defeated, in an irrevocable and definitive way. Already from the start he is vanquished, overcome and completely subjugated, willing to take the pain in every physical and spiritual way, to be frustrated and humiliated. From this he derives satisfaction. As the director of his own affliction, he transforms a potential enemy into an obedient and disciplined actress, into a student whose only task is learning the art of inflicting pain. That is why he binds her to him in the most underhanded and captious way, branding with his own stamp any eventual hostile drive, so that the woman can do anything except leave her servant. Around her have been placed not so much boundaries that she could overcome, as limits that are the conditions of the experience of betrayal. Even though she may couple with another man in front of him, he would still be the deus ex machina, the author of this scene. The contract opens a theatrical space beyond which no experiences are possible. To be sure, she could torment and torture him beyond all limits, but in so doing she would only be damaging her own slave, that is, a thing that belongs to her. The woman could break her contract and leave, but she would be giving up one of her possessions. The logic of masochism is not controlled at all by a neutral and impersonal movement. Its foundation is precisely the interest of the two contracting parties to draw up and maintain the contract. Certainly, masochism implies a deep experience of giving oneself as a thing and taking as a thing. The servant who offers himself in an unconditioned and absolute way treats his woman as a puppet in his power. The woman who accepts being the passive executrix of the representations planned by the servant knows very well that in them she has always the role of one who commands, disposes and possesses the body of the partner according to her own total will. But it is always a question of the interests of two subjects, two people, two contracting parties, and not of an impersonal, neutral and anonymous feeling. Masochism is a wile of subjectivity, not the sexual appeal of the inorganic. It anticipates what it is afraid of and in this manner hopes to neutralize it.

The question raised by masochism is whether it is not too clever, that is, if it does not end by provoking precisely what it fears. By believing that betrayal is inevitable and ineluctable, it attempts to exorcize it, by taking away the intoxication of the transgression and the aplomb of seriousness, making it mechanical and comical. From this point of view, it would seem that its motive is more the fear of pain than the pleasure of pain. But here an element intervenes, which like the spermaphogous breath, is at the same time physical, psychic and intellectual. The physical pain constitutes the guarantee that the excitement can always be renewed. We cannot access it directly because otherwise we would fall back into a naturalistic experience that privileges pleasure over pain, orgasm over expectation. Physical suffering constitutes an external leverage point, a mediation, a place of transit through which pass, at the same time, corporeal sensations, psychic humiliation and the intellectual awareness of one's own moral superiority. Precisely, this intermingling of different factors makes of masochism a sexual and theoretical construction, which for some aspects is similar to the sex appeal of the inorganic, not only as far as the aspiration to the perennial availability of excitement is concerned, or as far as the singular amalgam of bodily and philosophical solicitations, but also for the tendency to suspend the sexual act without precipitating it into a gratification that suddenly concludes the experience and leaves unsatisfied the will to let it last forever.

However, between masochism and the neutral and impersonal sexuality of the thing that feels there is a fundamental difference. The masochist moves along a vertical axis that connects the dignity and splendour of control to the baseness and degradation of submission. The masochist relation is a continuous up and down, a very swift succession of exaltations and disheartenments, and even a simultaneity of celebrations and insults, of apotheoses and humiliations, of gratuitous arrogance and unjustified feelings of guilt. Masochism takes its own nourishment from a very strong, irrepressible and uncontrollable aspiration toward excellence, supremacy, perfection. The man who is easily contented, who is indulgent toward himself and others, is a stranger to the tumultuous and dizzy experience of masochism, to the harsh mountainous landscape of peaks and chasms to which it introduces us. One should have been born a god to know the cruel happiness of masochism. That is why it is also attracted to the opposite pole, to the mistreated and suffering animal, to the wild and inhuman beast. The main character of the novel *Venus in Fur* is also a dangerous hyena. Severin, the protagonist of Masoch's novel, is both a deus ex machina of the entire plot and the beaten and kicked dog. Although violent, the masochist experience is neither traumatic, fatal, nor tragic. The real catastrophe is the failure, not the achievement of masochism. The masochist is not stupid, or someone who loves injury. He wants to win and triumph and to this end he adopts paradoxical techniques that restrain the partner within insuperable limits. He frames her, so to speak, in a scene from which she cannot escape. Within it she will act out the role of a sensual and cruel mistress but it is clear that she can be a Venus in fur only as long as she stays within the plot designed by Severin. If she were indeed to go against these limits, she will end up a poor woman, a wretch from whom the greatness of abjection is precluded. Unlike masochism, neutral sexuality is horizontal. It has nothing to do with the divine or with the animal world, rather with the artificial world of things that feel. It does not originate from the contradiction between excellence and degradation, but from the unconditional approval of the unlimited space opened up by the disappearance of the subject.

12

Bodies as Clothing

In the masochistic experience the attention devoted to clothing and to hairstyle is striking. The eccentric shopping, the purchase of unusual clothing, which reveals signs of superiority and social challenge, precede and prepare the masochistic sexual acts. Even the neutral and impersonal sexuality of the thing that feels institutes a relation with clothing, but the nature of this relationship is much more essential and different from both the aesthetic connection between beauty and sexual attraction, and from the masochistic connection between sensitive domination and splendour. The fact that a beautiful appearance arouses and favours a sexual approach seems an obvious fact connected with the very nature of man, if not, indeed, with a law of nature. A nice dress seems, in any case, the promise of a beautiful body. The fact that the promise is kept or not, that the dress anticipates or hides, is secondary with respect to the false evidence of a connection between beauty and sexuality.

In actuality, the aesthetic–sexual conception of clothing does not originate from an actual experience of clothing as such. The dress is subordinated to the beauty of the body and to its sexual attraction. As long as we remain prisoners of the idea that living bodies excite us more than clothes, we will never escape the organicistic aestheticism that considers sexuality in terms of life. It is not true that Western thought is characterized by a dualism between body and soul. Body and soul resemble each other too much to truly constitute an opposition. Those who today defend the rights of the body imagine it always as something living and animated, as a spirit that one can see and touch, taste and savour, lick and suck, not as a thing that feels. The spiritualistic sensualism of the current advocates of corporeity is not different from the devout palpitations of pious souls. They both ignore the experience of the thing, of clothing, of the body as clothing. An animal does not feel differently from an angel. The lust of an animal in heat, the desiring fervour of the devout, the refined taste of an aesthete all resemble each other in the fact of being on the side of lived experience, not on that of the sentient thing. The real opposition is not between body and soul, but between life and clothing.

What does it mean to feel one's body or that of others as clothing? If I think of the body as a cover and as a sheath of the soul, what interests me, generally, is not the first but the second, and the first only as protection or tomb of the other. Therefore, I do not succeed in grasping the body in its clothing exteriority, in its essential being thing, but only in its relation with respect to something else which is more vital and more important. Now I can even subvert this order and say that the body is more vital and more important in itself than the soul. In fact, I am still thinking of the soul, of life, and not of clothing or the thing. Even if we consider body and soul as two manifestations of the same substance, the latter is not essentially clothing but something that can have two attributes: spirituality and materiality. Thus, I raise the entire sensitive world to God, but I do not think of it in its impersonal and inorganic neutrality.

A vitalist premise that prevents feeling the body as thing is at the basis of the modern ideology of the emancipation of the senses and the liberation of the body. The idea that our body is simply the continuation and extension of the clothes we wear is easily deduced from an observation of the contemporary look. We owe to Walter Benjamin the connection between the sex appeal of the inorganic and fashion. But the experience of a neutral and inorganic sexuality is no longer suitable to fashion, a notion by now obsolete and antiquated, rather, to the look, understood as the culture of the body-clothing completely emancipated both from the conformism of haute couture and from the subjectivity of anti-fashion. In the look, in fact, the experience of clothing as body is prolonged, extended and radicalized in that of the body as clothing. Make-up, tattooing, gymnastics, hairdressing, dietetics, aerobics, bodybuilding, plastic surgery and genetic engineering are the next steps of a journey that leads to man almost thing.

This notwithstanding, all this technology is subordinated to the exaltation of an ethico–aesthetic ideal of the human figure, whether masculine or feminine, to the Faustian dream of eternal youth, to the model of the body as sensitive expression of the soul, as the place of encounter, harmonization and permeation between spirit and matter, and to an idea of beauty as something polished, vital and fresh. But can sexual and philosophical excess really recognize itself in this spiritualizing and soporific mawkishness that does not even get to the experience of pleasure, but stops on the threshold of gratification? In fact, contemporary spiritualist sensualism does not know what to do with either sexuality or philosophy, because they are both limit-experiences that imply a choice, and mark, irrevocably, a destiny. Spiritualistic sensualism is totally immersed in a horizon of fatuity, frivolity and affectedness. It accepts mediocrity for ease, the inability to take resolve for openness, superficiality for affability. The body as thing to which it aspires is never a real thing but only a parasitic sub-product of the organic. Thus, the look is trampled under the chariot of idealizing and conciliatory aestheticism and everything collapses in amusing and futile banality.

And yet, in the look is implicit another intention that appears when its fundamental reifying inspiration can be manifested in its full autonomy, without being obliged to imitate the natural models of beauty, to make the old look young, to smooth away wrinkles from worn faces, and to redesign figures made heavy by cellulite. All that belongs to punk, to the hairdos of unnatural colours, to the neo-baroque taste for the funerary, to the torn clothes where cloth and skin alternate, all this belongs without doubt to the sex appeal of the inorganic and represents the contemporary triumph of that cadaverous and ghostly look in which Walter Benjamin discovered the very essence of fashion.

Even the provocation actualized by computer graphics that invent, by means of small subsequent variations, faces that have never existed in nature and cannot exist, belongs to the same sensibility that is aroused by a device pushed to the extreme and emancipated by any reference to an original model. This sensibility, in fact, no longer belongs to man but to the post-human horizon opened up by the union of philosophy and sexuality. The philosophy of the thing frees sexuality from its dependency on the organic, in which both psychoanalysis and feminism have kept it and, vice versa, neutral sexuality frees philosophy from the pale vitalist spiritualism in which both ethics and aesthetics keep it enclosed. This double emancipation occurs under the sign of body-clothing, of the look. Finally, the beauty of bodies, their masculine and feminine gender, their age no longer have any importance. What counts is their disposition and attitude to covering and being covered, to dressing and being dressed, to wrapping and being wrapped by fleshy tissues that have nothing organic any more, that cannot be distinguished from the clothing, the materials that usually hide them. Now to all this one arrives by means of philosophy. It seems to me impossible that any part of the human body seen as clothing can give excitement, certainly and infinitely, if one lacks the aware-ness of the excess in which I find myself thrown. The experience of the skin and the body as a totality of tissues is for its exterior-ity as opposite as one can get with respect to ethico-aesthetic sensualist spiritualism.

When your partner sinks his fingers in your vagina or when the lips of your mistress bare the penis, don't be excited by the old-fashioned idea that your body is reanimating and coming to life again, but by that more actual idea that you are sentient clothing! This way, there is no longer any interruption, any hiatus between you and feeling. Don't bank on a life that comes and goes, but on a tissue from which none can separate you. Perhaps you are afraid that this tissue now listens, now does not – that something could anaesthetize it. If so, you are still imagining yourself as an organ that lives or dies, is awake or asleep, and not as clothing. The excitement, in fact, is no longer thought of as something that is added to your body. It is the very same idea of being clothing to provoke excitement, to reawaken sensitivity, to make you travel in the neutral and impersonal territory of a sexuality without subject, without soul and without vital body. The sex appeal of the inorganic stands on philosophy, on attitude, on a habit of thinking the extreme, just as, vice versa, philosophy is driven on its autonomous journey of anonymous feeling, without gender, without face and without age, which surrounds us and envelops us. Philosophy, free from natural, organic sexuality, discovers the sexual virtuality of the look and, vice versa, the look frees philosophy from ethical and aesthetic sensualist sensualism.

13

Hegel and the Thing as 'not this'

No one shows better than Hegel how perceptive sensualism is foreign to the experience of the thing, for which sensible certainty is as abstract and universal as one can get. We believe mistakenly that the senses guarantee us a concrete and determinate experience. In actual fact, in the here and now of immediate feeling, the given constantly vanishes and is incessantly replaced by another given. The body that I hold firmly in my arms, from the moment in which it is given to me as a thing, ceases to be a particular object and becomes, rather, a 'not this', and eludes all specific determinations. Its essence is that of being mine. It is nothing outside of the fact of offering itself unconditionally to my possession and control. I fully accept the responsibility that comes from its giving itself, I take it and I support it. But I do not have anything definite. It is a matter of indifference that this body that gives itself without limitations is made a certain way, that it presents certain characteristics, has these breasts, these thighs, these hips. In fact all determinations disappear in its universal giving of itself. My knowledge of it is the simplest one can imagine. It is nothing but its being offered here and now to my possession. Its existence is not gathered up in an object, rather it overflows back and forth, up and down, right and left, extends, continues and disperses on the sheets, on the table, on the floor. The body as thing is annulled as body, it passes in a non-body, it travels in an empty and external universality, of which all that is relevant is the fact that it offers itself to sensation, here and now.

On the other hand, not only is my lover's body a thing, that is, neither this nor that, and susceptible of being this and that, but also mine is equally a sentient thing that gives itself and takes. The immediacy of my seeing, touching, licking does not authorize me to be posited as a unity, an identity, a subject. My I is no more essential than the thing that I hold. It too, is a 'not this', a simple and indifferent universal that slips away toward any other immediacy. The sentient thing that I am perceives in a neutral, impersonal, anonymous way. It is not I that feel, and it is perfectly indifferent to me to feel this or that, because the sentient thing that I am is all in the here and now, and in the continuous sliding from a this to another this.

This neutral sexuality, without determination and quality, for which all the functions of the flesh are the same because they are reduced to the simple immediacy of the unconditional give and take, seems the poorest that can be imagined. Colours, odours, flavours, forms, the copious and opulent exuberance of the vital world, everything is gradually denied by another immediacy that takes the place of the preceding one. The sex appeal of the inorganic is beyond any taste and distaste. Its excitement does not derive from sensitive properties that one experiences, as in natural sexuality ('it is rigid, pointed, big, hard and round,/ ladies, the pole that I plant in the ground', as Tansillo would say)[4], but from a movement that continuously overcomes the single sensitive given in an infinite pointing and denying. Under this aspect, the female sex seems closer to the essence of the thing than the male sex. In the continued pointing now to this fold and prominence of the vulva now to that one, now to this, now to that gorge and recess of the vagina, and in entrusting it to the fingers, the tongue, the penis of those she loves, the woman reveals a field of mountainous and uneven flesh, whose feeling is continuously changing. It gives itself as the reproduction in miniature of the whole world, as an extremely irregular inorganic nature, as a landscape made of uneven, rough surfaces, mountains, rocks, precipices that now feel, now do not, now cry, now are silent, now they abandon themselves to a tumultuous perturbation, now they remain arid and motionless. But the continuous variability of the sensitive point, its continuous transfer from one place to another, its unceasing drifting through this or that fold, this and that peak, this and that curve, makes it possible for the indication of the place that, here and now, it is about to feel, is at the same time a denial of what it felt in the previous moment and now no longer does.

The abstract and indeterminate character of the feeling of the thing makes it so that what is essential is not lying but denying. The here and now of excitement never stops, it is always in transit towards another place, cannot recognize itself in what has been, and can only preserve itself in the form of an affirmation that denies – of a denial, precisely. Generally, one considers denial as the opposite of being coherent, as self-contradiction, as recantation of what one has said before, as not abiding by the word and the image one gave. But is not this way of considering denial a victim of that logic of identity that sensible certainty – precisely – dissolves? Generally, denial means not abiding by expectation, to disappoint the promise. But, in so doing, we forget that denial is something positive, is the opposite of the lie. If I say 'not this', it is because I am avoiding the ethico–aesthetic sensualism which pretends that bodies and souls are in possession of stable and permanent qualities. Perhaps souls and bodies have actually a firm and fixed identity, but not things. If I say 'not this', it is because I am not interested in the liveliness of this soul, or the beauty of this body, but only in the abstract universality of the sentient thing. It is not in the manifold world of life, or in the grandeur of forms that my excitement originates, but, on the contrary, in the fact that both the life of the souls as the form of the bodies are negated by a broader and more extreme affirmation, which does not stop at any spiritual or sensible determination, is not blocked by the enchantment of a look or by the gentleness of a caress, but denies them and perseveres in giving itself as a universal thing that here and now is capable of feeling and making feel all. Paradoxically, it is precisely denial, which does not stop before the this, which guarantees and protects the infinity of excitement.

14

Fetishism and Sex Appeal
of the Inorganic

Fetishism is the category under which modern culture, during the last two centuries, has thought of the impersonal and neutral sexuality of the thing that feels. It has constituted both a misunderstanding and an acknowledgement of the phenomenon which is the subject of our study. On the one hand, the fetish is a caricature of the sex appeal of the inorganic, of which it offers a grotesque and extravagant version, on the other hand, it possesses those requisites that shed light on the issue of the relation between philosophy and sexuality that only today it is possible fully to grasp and develop.

This ambiguity is clear ever since the origins of the notion of fetishism which, as is well-known, are to be found in the anthropology of religion of the second half of the eighteenth century. For Charles de Brosses, the author of *Du culte des dieux fétiches*, fetishism represents the most primitive and coarse form of religion. He opposes this notion to Platonic representational art, which sees in the religion and in the mythology of the ancients the indirect and allegorical expression of pure and abstract intellectual ideas. In his view, instead, the cults of all primitive people, in which he includes the Egyptians as well as his contemporary Black Americans and American Indians, address particular things, which are worshipped in their single specificity.

What characterizes the fetish from a general point of view is its arbitrariness. Unlike the idol which is representational, that is, the image of a divine being, the fetish does not represent and does not reproduce anything. It gives itself here and now in its being thing, in its abstract universality that completely leaves out of consideration any relation with a spirit or a determined form. It is neither the symbol, nor the sign, nor the figure of something else, but is valid solely for itself, in its splendid independence and autonomy. Fetishism, therefore, is the opposite of idolatry. While the latter is in agreement with the ethico–aesthetic sensualist idealism, with the exalting of specific qualities, with the celebration of this or that sensitive or supersensitive entity, spiritual or natural, fetishism marks the triumph of the artificial which is actually offered in its opaque and indifferent arbitrariness, in its being a sentient thing. Anything can become a fetish: a rock, a lock of hair, a tone of voice, an odour, a word, or a colour. Starting from the moment when it ceases to be the object identical to itself of the perception of a subject, and is free of any other relation with the other from itself, the fetishist thing acquires a dizzy universality that de Brosses has been able to capture even if in a critical and disparaging way. In short, the fetish is not a god or a goddess of Greek polytheism, is not the product of the deification of a mode of being human, it is not the materialization of an ideal of perfection. On the contrary, it is aniconic, imageless and alien from any qualitative sensuality. If anything can become a fetish, all fetishes can stop being such. Fetishism does not open any pantheon, but transits from entity to entity, investing with its relentless reifying universality, with its greatest tangible abstraction, plants and animals, men and stones, sounds, colours, tastes, sensations, experiences, ideas, sentiments, passions. The choice made by the fetishist device is merely casual. Here lies its strength with respect to idolatry. It does not worship the world, has no illusions about it, and yet it declares itself, without reservations and with the greatest energy, in favour of a part, a detail, a specific circumstance, leaving to it all its tangible and groundless factuality. One could even state that fetishism contains more contempt than admiration for the natural world as a whole. In fact, the unconditional reverence with which it considers an accidental entity is so illegitimate, capricious and irregular, as to reveal disrespect and contempt for the order and organic unity of the cosmos.

The second specific character of fetishism is its externality. This aspect is placed in evidence above all by Kant whose point of view on fetishism is even more critical and polemical than de

Brosses's. For Kant, fetishism is not opposed to the idol but to moral faith. While the latter has its own foundation in itself, fetishism is connected to a servile worship so rendered for external reasons that leaves out of consideration the obligation of pure moral duty. For Kant, one encounters a fetishistic cult every time that the essence of religion is singled out in statutory commandments, in external rules, in observances functional to reaching a certain purpose, as when one establishes a church, a priesthood, a religious institution which claims to do away with reason and sets itself up as sole guardian, and authorized interpreter of God's will. For Kant, therefore, on the one hand, fetishism crosses into magic, which pretends to act on God to achieve effects in the world that man by himself cannot create. On the other hand, it crosses into ecclesiastic theocracy which is the instrument through which the clergy rules and dictates without the need of having to persuade. Fetishism, thus, is the object of a double condemnation. A moral one in the name of a purity of faith, according to a perspective inspired by the Protestant Reformation, and a political condemnation in the name of the invisible church implicit in natural religion, according to a perspective inspired by the Enlightenment. Although Kant denies to fetishism any philosophical dignity, one could ask whether a consideration of rituals, ceremonies, institutions, in short, of the external aspect of religion, which frees it from magic and from politics, from superstition and from power, would have been the subject of such a categorical rejection. In fact, what seems essential to me in fetishism is not so much the search for divine favour through external practices, as the attraction that these practices exercise in themselves, independently of the fact of being the instruments of a utilitarian subjectivity that calculates and employs even the divine as means for attaining one's own purposes. Ritual can also be appreciated and evaluated in itself, without resorting to an external support that founds it and legitimizes it. The religion of ancient Rome is an example of a ritual without myth, of a cult without images and without idols, whose effectiveness is essentially turned toward the historical world of legal and social relations. The word 'thing' derives from the Latin *causa*, which means both what provokes an effect, and the totality of disputes on which the judge gives his opinion. Now the fetish is rather a 'cause in itself' separate from the effect, indifferent with respect to judgement. In the effect the cause is no longer such, but crosses into something else, just as in sentencing the prosecution of a trial is resolved in a univocal solution. To be sure, from Kant's point of view, for whom the cause and effect relation is a condition of experience that can never be disavowed at the level of phenomenal reality, the auto-nomization of the cause is an absurdity. But Kant does not exclude the possibility of thinking things according to relations independent of mechanism. The alternative to the latter, however, is finalism, whereby things are organized in view of a general and global order. Now it is clear that in a teleological conception of the world or of society, fetishism disappears. Its place is taken by the totem, namely, a thing that does not count in itself, but as an emblem of a social group and guarantee of its organic unity.

Symbology in the sciences of religion and totemism in anthropology put an end, in the twentieth century, to the scandal of fetishism. They inserted the thing in an organized complex, in a totality, whether metaphysical or social, from which it obtains a reasonable result and a precise function. But the fetish is precisely the negation of symbol and totem. It consists in the insubordination of the thing with respect to the living organism, to the system, to the structure that purports to absorb it. Therefore, one assigns to the fetish the stature of a unique, irregular, marginal thing. It is a remainder, an anomaly, a dead head (*caput mortuum*), entirely secondary and irrelevant with respect to the functioning of society.

Fetishism, expelled by the primitive world, had its triumphal entrance into the economy and psychology of the contemporary world with Marx and Freud, respectively. For the former, the fetish is not the product of the extravagant imagination of some people cut off from progress or belonging to a remote past, but, on the contrary, it constitutes an essential aspect of commodities and money. In primitive and medieval economies, the thing is not a fetish because it counts for its qualities, for its use value, for its sensible characteristics. It is only from the moment that it is introduced essentially as commodity, that it is endowed with an exchange value, that it becomes an enigma, a hieroglyph, 'a thing sensibly oversensible',[5] because it unites in itself the concrete aspect connected to its being somewhat usable and the abstract aspect connected with its being somewhat exchangeable with any other commodity. Marx, therefore, gives to commodity the character of fetish because in it one can find both the universal arbitrariness remarked by de Brosses, and the autonomous exteriority emphasized by Kant. Commodification submits the object of use to a strange metamorphosis that makes it more philosophical, because it liberates it from a qualitative concreteness, from the fact of being only the receptacle of human sensations, and more sexual, because it attributes to it a sensory quality independent of man so that sociability acquires the aspect of a relation between things rather than between subjects. However, we must not forget that the fetishism of commodity is an illusion, a fantastic figure that veils and hides the reality of value production. The latter is not at all arbitrary or external and depends exclusively on the amount of time of human labour. In short, Marx is not interested so much in the fetishist enigma of commodity *per se*, as in the unveiling of its mystery, the liberation from the spell that leads men to attribute to things an exchange value independent of labour, that makes them assign the origins of the exchange value of commodities to natural factors rather than to social ones. Whoever seeks the value of commodities in the qualitative character of objects becomes a victim of idolatrous deceit, and reasons as physiocrats did who thought that land revenue came from nature and not from society. Under this aspect Marx opens the way to the sex appeal of the inorganic to the extent that he clears up the ethico–aesthetic sensualist idealism which praises, applauds and honours the beauty of the world, the splendour of objects, the enjoyment of forms, ignoring or keeping quiet the fact that in bourgeois society everything is branded by the stamp of alienated labour, everything is commodity, everything is not a useless and unreal abstraction, but, on the contrary, greatly effective, operative, sensible. Speaking against the idolatry of commodities, Marx captures, in spite of himself, the dizzy universality and autonomy of the sex appeal of the inorganic, which is implicit, therefore, in every aspect of capitalist reality. In this society, it is no longer possible to be pleasure-loving in an immediate and naive way without seeming vulgar and showy. Whoever appreciates objects for their natural qualities, forgetting that they are essentially commodities, that is, products of abstract labour, is blinded by a glitter that does not belong to the world of the spirit or to life but to the inorganic world of things understood as things. One enters this horizon by linking the abstraction of philosophy to the neutral and impersonal feeling of inorganic sexuality. Philosophy without sexuality reveals the mystery of commodity, but is not able to love it as such and therefore decays in a knowledge which is sad and melancholy. Sexuality without philosophy remains enclosed in the contradictions of fetishism and is incapable, therefore, of passing from nature to artifice, from orgasm to the sex appeal of the inorganic.

Beside commodities, the other economic entity to which Marx assigns the character of fetish is financial capital, because it appears as something independent and personal, endowed with a life of its own and autonomous with respect to labour, which, instead, is the true origin of its growth. The monetary capital that can be lent valorizes itself, that is creates interest through a movement in which any mediation is cancelled. It reaches the pure form of fetish because any ambiguity as to the formal quality, the use value, the sensible aspect of the commodity is lacking. It is a totally abstract supercommodity, which by the sole fact of being lent produces an increase proportional to the time after which it is surrendered. The formula M-M' (money creates money) seems to annul the movement of production and circulation. Labour and exchange disappear in the illusion of a movement in which capital is preserved and reproduced completely aside from the manner in which it is effectively used by the person to whom it is lent. The person, as a rule, will function as an active agent of production, that is, as an industrial capitalist who obtains from the capital he was lent a profit greater than the interest he has to pay. But since the rate of profit is less certain than the rate of interest, and since the debtor could also be a squanderer, one disregards all actions and social relations connected with the actual investment of the capital borrowed. The financial capital, thus, takes on the appearance of a fetish, of a thing that has absorbed any social relation and that in this radical exteriorization erases and renders unrecognizable all transits, transformations and the mediation necessary to its growth. In short, it seems that capital itself has become an autonomous and natural source of profit that reproduces spontaneously.

What relation is there between the fetishism of the financial capital and the sex appeal of the inorganic? Or better, how can the fetishism of borrowed money constitute an imaginary, symbolic, emotional reference point for the philosophical sexuality of the thing that feels? This relation is once again ambiguous and distorted but not without a lesson to teach. In Pauline Réage's novel, *L'Histoire d'O*, a man called René lends his mistress willingly to a number of people unknown to her, who rape and torture her, for the sole purpose of obtaining from this experiment a surplus of excitement for himself. The fact that others may temporarily do to her what they want constitutes for him the proof that she belongs to him, because one can lend only what belongs to one. The woman in question known by the letter O, constitutes, precisely, a fetish of sexual excitement similar to financial capital that grows only to the extent in which it is temporarily alienated. Analogously to financial capital, René does not add anything of his to the process of valorization of capital and expects that this work be done by others. This relation lacks reciprocity completely because René, who poses as the master of O, does not expose himself to a process of de-subjectification and reification and, even though he is dependent on a third character, a certain Sir Stephen, he lives this subjection in a purely psychic and spiritual way. The story of O demonstrates well the ambiguity of fetishism. It consists in the separation, the hiatus, the conflict between the capitalist and his capital, between René who occupies the role of the master and O who lives an adventure of extreme degradation without rebelling. The relation between the two is determined by the challenge that O presents to her lover and that she succeeds in winning through imaginary devices that belong to the divine and bestial world, but not to the neutral and impersonal world of the thing that feels. In the last scene of the novel, during which O with her face covered with an owl mask is brought in naked on a leash tied to a chain hooked to a ring that perforates the lips of her sex, he ordains her a goddess and humiliates her as an animal, but does not legitimate her as a thing that feels. It is as if the divine and natural world still always interferes in a project that concerns, instead, the world of things. Economic fetishism cannot think of commodity and money as things. They are either divinities or monsters.

In anthropological and economical reflections on fetishism is inherent the idea that it is the substitute, the surrogate, the deceitful double of something true and essential. The religious fetish is in the place of God, the economical one replaces and hides the use value of human labour. Something dead, inorganic, and past arrogates the right to a sentient existence. It is an absolutely inadmissible claim which, therefore, is the object of a condemnation without appeal. This characteristic of fetishism is emphasized and underlined by psychoanalysis, which considers it, however, as the substitute not of something that is there, but of an entirely imaginary entity, the female penis. According to Freud, the origin of fetishism must be sought in childhood trauma. Even though reality shows the child the lack of phallus in the female anatomy, he refuses to give up his original conviction which also attributes a phallus to the female sex, and places this absence in relation to the fear of castration from which he feels directly threatened. There arise in him, therefore, two contradictory psychic demands. On the one hand, he cannot deny the evidence that the woman lacks the penis, on the other hand, he cannot abandon his belief that protects him from the threat of castration. He elaborates, therefore, a compromise between these two opposite psychic necessities, attributing to the woman a substitute penis, a fetish precisely, which can be any object whatever, such as a shoe, or a part of her body, her feet, on which he focuses his sexual interest. This process is made possible by a division in the self, part of which denies the evidence. To define this process, Freud elaborates the concept of negation (*Verleugnung*). Fetishism, therefore, would be a psychic device that makes possible the negation of sexual difference, even though recognizing it partially. It implies a relation of substantial extraneity with respect to the real female sex.

And what if negation, which according to Freud is at the basis of fetishism, did not concern the supposed evidence of female sexuality, but the existence of a neutral and impersonal sexuality? In other words, what if the fetish were not born from the negation of femininity, but from the sex appeal of the inorganic? What if the fetish were the substitute not for the penis, but for the thing that feels? Freud has expressly recognized that the elaboration of his theory depends essentially on the study of male sexuality. Therefore, he has remained prisoner of a naturalistic model of sexuality that, even being completely emancipated by the traditional notion of subject, nonetheless understands dynamic processes as impulses, vital drives oriented towards the abolition of excitement and states of tension. Beside this notion of drive oriented toward complete discharge, there is in Freud's work another idea of drive directed toward the preservation of a constant level of excitement, his theory of homeostasis. This theory seems more to conform to the experience of the neutral sexuality of the thing that feels, which rests, precisely, on prolonging excitement for an indeterminate time. But we must not forget that Freud's thought does not escape the vitalistic premise that makes him view the inorganic as synonymous with death and destruction, as reduction of all tensions to zero and as the dissolution of all ties.

It is meaningful, however, that fetishism does not find a place in his analysis of the death drive. In fact, the fetish remains connected to a surplus of excitement which is not without a relation to negation and the division of the self. Fetishism gives woman an impersonal phallus, characterized by a universal arbitrariness and an autonomous exteriority, a shoe, a piece of clothing or glove taking the place of what she lacks. This substitute is a phallus without quality, without determinations, it is an improper phallus, a thing that excites not for its symbolism, and not even because it represents some part of the natural body, male or female, but because it constitutes an addition, a non-essential appendix that holds within itself and almost monopolizes the entire feeling. The fetishist is excited by the fact of being felt by a thing to which he attributes the feeling of his mistress, who, for this reason, is virtually excluded from the experience. The implicit discourse that the fetishist proposes to her goes like this: 'I lend you what you are missing, that is an organ that feels me. It does not matter that you through this substitution do not feel anything, because what counts is that I feel that it feels me. This indirect impression gives me a surplus that adds to my direct excitement.' In Junichiro Tanizaki's novel, *The Key* (*Kagi*), a foot fetish plays, in fact, the role of stimulating the sexual life of the protagonist. It is practised on his wife who, initially, is rather cold and incapable of feeling in an autonomous way.

The fetishist, vice versa, can also lend his woman to a foreign phallus with which he identifies in his imagination, in order to obtain from this exchange a surplus of excitement for himself. Tanizaki's novel moves precisely in this direction. The husband is attracted by his wife to the extent that he can identify with the foreign eye of another, to whom he assigns the task of developing the pictures of his naked wife. But in this case what plays the role of the fetish? Is the entire body of this third man the substitute, not for the husband's penis, but for his wife's? However, in Tanizaki's novel, it does not present those characteristics of universal arbitrariness and autonomous exteriority that are essential to fetishism. In this direction, but in a much more radical way, Pierre Klossowski has gone in his trilogy *Les lois de l'hospitalité*. Here fetishism is institutionalized, so to speak, in the anonymous figure of the guest, to whom the husband offers his own wife not only to receive confirmation of his own mastery over her, but also to derive from his own identification with the guest a surplus of excitement. The main character of Klossowski's novel is, after all, the example par excellence of a division in the self. He succeeds in being at the same time both host and guest, both husband and lover. It is precisely on this duplicity that the entire fetishist strategy is founded.

From a general point of view, it seems that the Freudian theory of fetishism is based on the premise of feminine frigidity, lesser or greater, true or simulated, as it may be. In fact, the women in these two novels, Ikiuko and Roberte, are austere women, the first because of a rigid traditional education, the second because of her political militancy and her participation in a censorship committee. If we place this premise aside, what is left of psychoanalytical fetishism? To be sure, the theory of negation and division of the self have many points in common with anthropological and economic fetishism. They constitute a development of those characteristics of universal arbitrariness, autonomous exteriority, sensible annulment of qualities and profit of a surplus of excitement that can also be found in de Brosses, Kant and Marx.

Since fetishism is, among the so-called perversions, the one that seems the closest to the sex appeal of the inorganic, I cannot conclude this chapter without alluding to fetishist love. It seems to me different from the three great forms of love developed in the West: medieval courtly love, the love-passion of the Baroque and Romantic love. Love has always been connected with the experience of a despairing causality and arbitrariness. It has always remained incomprehensible why one chooses this person and not another as the object of absolute and exclusive sexual, emotional and intellectual investment. But in previous historical forms, the moral and sensual elements, that is the spirit and life, played such an important role that they overshadowed the empty accidentality of being thing. In short, one thought of loving someone because of certain moral and physical qualities, and ethical and aesthetic idealism ruled even when it took on the aspect of spells and incantations. Instead, when one feels infinitely attracted and indissolubly tied to a partner, above all and first of all, for the empty and external universality of its flesh covering, for the abstract impersonality of its unlimited give and take, for the enigmatic process through which something anonymous, indeterminable, neutral stops at a corporeal clothing without attributing to it any intrinsic value, what wins out and triumphs is a sense of inexorable dependency with respect to the super-thing that one succeeded in being, and with respect to the superthing in which one was able to tranform oneself. Strange fidelity is what is impossible to escape. It is born from being resigned to having what one cannot deprive oneself of, but with which one would also like to do without. The exclusiveness of fetishist love does not stand on the confirmation of positive requisites, but, paradoxically, on denial, on negation. She or he are neither this nor that, but neither not this nor not that. Fetishist love opens us up on a reification of the entire cosmos, of which this body that I embrace and penetrate is, so to speak, the irreplaceable replacement. It feels me here and now, and always returns to me augmented by the feeling that I am also for it the irreplaceable replacement. The encounter between an artificial sexuality and a reified philosophy generates an excitement which, just as financial capital, is preserved and always returns a little richer. Fetishist love, unlike mystical love, is a rich love. It does not propose, at all, that model of adamitic 'nudity' which is at the basis of spiritual dispossession. The suspension of all purposes, the annulment of the sensible world, the disappearance of subjectivity lead to results opposite to those reached through mysticism. Not the union with an original source, but dependency with regard to the substitute.

15

Hardcore Sonority

Beside the neutral excitement of drugs, sci-fi futurism and the radical exteriority of the look, rock music constitutes another fundamental aspect of impersonal feeling in our time. In order to arrive at comprehending the sexually inorganic character of rock, it is necessary to free oneself of the sentimental conception of music, which considers it as the expression of an emotional interiority, and from the vitalistic one which sees in it the animal cry, the spontaneous manifestation of natural existence. The essence of music is neither sentiment nor life, but more essentially, *sound*, understood precisely in the neutral and inorganic indifference evoked by this word.

Schelling is the philosopher who has underlined this character of music, defining it as the inorganic form of art par excellence. One could say that music is thing, both when it appears as discontinuous sonority, and when it is an interrupted stretch of sonority. Music is connected to the most elementary level of physicality with a corporeity which is not animal, but rather that of heavenly bodies. Referring back to the well-known Pythagorean theory, Schelling claims that the movements of the stars do not cause music but are themselves music. Music is not so much a technique, that is the product of human action, as it is a given, a thing, an already real entity that does not need either human spirituality or human industry. The body and the soul, the voice and the instrument are subordinate to music. They become music only when they conform to the inorganicity of the thing, repressing the eccentric singularity of a song that pretends to be the expression of a sentient subjectivity, or the whimsicality of a sound that claims primacy only by virtue of the fact of being produced by an instrument. To be sure, all music, and not song alone, has for Schelling a relation with self-awareness, in fact, in his view, it is the real self-numbering of the soul. But this numeration is unconscious. Through it, the subject reaches that union of abstraction and actuality which is typical of numeric reification, of economic quantification. Certainly, for Schelling, all music and not only the instrumental type, has cosmic meaning. Music forms are the forms of being of heavenly bodies as such. But the mineral and inorganic character of music does not exclude the existence of an opaque and impersonal feeling that belongs to it essentially. In fact, music is a type of spoken but not living word, something similar to a petrified god transformed into thing.

The fact that music is a sentient thing is shown by a series of research and sound experiences that belong to the world of rock. Starting from Total music at the end of the 1960s, through meta-rock, futurist rock, cosmic music, new-wave, hardcore and industrial music, it seems that rock has become emancipated bit by bit from the dimension of the word and sentimental and expressive living action, to reveal itself as the most widespread and emblematic cultural manifestation of neutral feeling, of a sex appeal of the extreme inorganic. Under many aspects, the adventure of progressive rock constitutes a paradigm for the cultural operations to come. The planetary character, the liberation from ties with different genres, the decision to mix the most diverse forms in a total experience, the will to provoke an artificial excitement different from everything offered from nature, turns progressive rock into a model in which creative philosophy recognizes itself with enthusiasm and wonder.

Already in the idea of Total music, announced by Frank Zappa, of a sound landscape in which the differences between classical and popular sound, avant-garde and commercial production, music and noise are collapsed, one can discover the fundamental intuition that excites inorganic sexuality. It depends entirely on the answer that we are able to give to these questions: 'Why is it that what is many-coloured, broken, not put together in an organic and coherent unity, holds together and does not dissolve in a senseless and deformed mass?' 'What distinguishes the inorganic from the disorganic, the pile, the mess?' 'If everything is sound, all is well?' No, on the contrary. Although the values of ethical and aesthetic idealism are entirely inadequate, there is another criterion which is more rigorous than manners and good taste. Its character is more essentially philosophical and has to do with the coherence, the courage, the determination of going with serenity and self-confidence to the extreme consequences of the journey one has undertaken. This is the only philosophical method, its procedure, the journey of life to which it points, not the construction of a cage, or the endless and inconclusive discussion on the conditions of the validity of judgements. From the moment that philosophy ceases to be the servant of ethics and aesthetics, good manners and good taste, it finds in progressive rock an encouragement to continue along the journey on which it has already been twice, in antiquity after the condemnation of Socrates and, in the modern period, after Bruno's murder.

But I have not yet answered the question on the difference between inorganic and disorganic. It is simple: only the inorganic is sexy and philosophical. Only the inorganic is essentially musical. In fact, it is held together by a power of cohesion that Schelling calls 'magnetism' and which represents the activity of the inorganic world. Sound, in his view, depends entirely on cohesion, and resounding is nothing other than the affirmation of cohesion. If this tonic force implicit in the world of things did not exist, maybe the world would fall apart, would be undone and would dissolve in an abyssal silence. Music, in its substance, is what holds and keeps it together.

The relation of sound and sex is conditioned by the existence of a force of attraction that unites them and which is neither spiritual nor animal. The sex appeal of the inorganic acts like a magnet. I feel attracted by the body of my lover as a piece of iron by a magnet, so that, each time, it is always only a pull that succeeds in interrupting the contact of our bodies. The spiritual metaphor of a union is no more adequate than that of the animal with hunger and thirst. On careful examination, sexual embrace does not establish and does not realize a unity, or ever fulfil or satisfy a need. The magnet establishes a permanent field of attraction, a continuity of forces that variously intersect. In the end, there is no substantial difference between feeling filled by the breath of one's lover and plunging into the depths of her cavities, to the point of feeling that the penis and the finger that penetrate at the same time the vagina and the anus, respectively, almost end up touching, separated only by a thin layer that divides them internally. Now philosophy and music are a kind of reassurance of this continuity that makes it possible for lovers to be always immersed in the magnetic field of reciprocal attraction.

That music has a closer relation with space than with time, as many aesthetic theories from Hegel to Stravinsky and beyond have tried to connect it, can appear odd at first. And yet, as long as we privilege the temporal dimension, we remain caught within a conceptual horizon characterized by reference to inwardness, to consciousness and to the subject, rather than to accessibility, outwardness and the neutral. On the other hand, the supremacy of the spatiality of music over temporality seems connected to a series of practices linked to technological innovation, such as recording and the manipulation of sounds and noises, the emphasis on environmental background sound, and the use of the synthesizer as lead instrument. These activities have generally led to a greater use of electronics in music production, as well as, with Brian Eno, to the creation of an environmental music in which the places themselves are endowed with a sonority that should belong to them in a continuous and persistent way.

An analogous shift from the primacy of temporality to that of spatiality has occurred in philosophical reflection where the notions of spatial presence, openness and network, have led to an ontological topology oriented to assigning to technology a recognition and an appreciation far greater than those offered by spiritualist philosophies, centred on the experience of lived time.

And more generally, sexuality, music and philosophy meet in promoting the shift from a horizon of lack, precariousness and rarity of experience, linked to the inexorable flow of time, to a horizon of availability, of immediate use, open to the possibility of gaining access to a spatial offer always virtually present. Even in this case one has to underscore a complete inversion of tendency with respect to the cult of those rare privileged moments to which those highly strung and thoughtful people in the nineteenth century and in the first half of the twentieth century devoted themselves. Those moments of rare spirituality or of animal frenzy that they allowed themselves from time to time seem to us a source of disappointment, frustration and failure. Neutral sexuality, progressive rock and the philosophy of transit convince us to be suspicious of the time of the spirit and of life because they do not keep their promises and plunge those who trust them into the diabolical and death. Instead, the sex appeal of the inorganic relies on the generous and hospitable spatiality of the world of things – bodies, sounds and thoughts – that infinitely welcome us with unlimited accessibility.

For the neutral sexuality of the thing that feels, concepts such as independence of the individual, autonomy of the person, freedom of the subject are words devoid of meaning because body and soul are constituted in their identity only by removing themselves definitively from the magnetism of inorganic cohesion, only by ceasing to be things, to become spirit and life. Nothing, writes Schelling, has the reason of its own existence within itself. It is meaningless to say: '*keep centred*', 'become self-sufficient', 'conquer your autonomy', because the sentient thing exists only to be attracted, called, drawn by the magnet to which it is destined to adhere. Therefore, the sex appeal of the inorganic is different from apparently similar notions such as seduction, which entails the working out of a strategy, or glamour, which is worked out through the spell of the look, or as charm which refers back to the enchantment of repetition, rituals and ceremonies. German cosmic music, for instance the work of Klaus Schulze, by re-creating electronically the effects of Wagner's infinite melody, offers at times a sonorous equivalent of a sexual feeling characterized essentially by the experience of an inorganic attraction. In music, excitement is infinite insofar as it is artificial, entirely entrusted to synthesizers that create new unheard-of sounds. Similarly, the persistence of sexual tension depends on the disappearance of the spiritual and the natural, both replaced by the abstract reification of bodies almost become stars, which as a result of magnetic forces cannot go too far from one another. As for philosophy, what makes it so fatal is not the fact of being, as Heidegger says, 'the seamstress of the stars'.[6]

The fact is that progressive rock, inorganic sexuality and the philosophy of the thing meet in the hard core of a common experience that consists in transferring feeling from man to things. This does not mean that man does not feel at all, in fact, this neutral and impersonal feeling is extremely intense but it does not belong to him any more. A type of devolution, transference, passing of feeling takes place from the subject to something completely external that can appear now as cosmos, now as technological apparatus, now as culture, now as market. The devolution, however, is not an involution. No return is possible to the primitive, the original, the natural. The horizon opened by devolution is posthuman not prehuman. The *hardcore* of progressive rock's sonority does not consist in the delirious performance of shouts, sexual breathing and moans, accompanied by a *heavy metal* instrumental approach, but in the fact that both the human voice and the sounds of instruments are accessible only through a distortion, a filter, a montage that renders them artificial, but not mechanical. Somehow, these sounds are harmonized on a neutral sensibility which, because it evades both pleasure and pain, knows no rest and no catharsis.

Thus the electronic manipulation of the human voice evokes infinite penetrations that go beyond the mouth and the throat into depths that are no longer flesh. It is as if the very chanting of things were coming from these invasions into channels that resemble more organ pipes than biological ducts. Thus, the adulteration of the sound of musical instruments by means of the synthesizer celebrates continuous and total touching and sucking. It is as if from contact, from the unruly and uncontrolled handling of limbs that only seem glued to the rest of the body, were to emerge the very sonority of the real. Technologization and industrialization reveal the essentially musical character of things which, however, does not depend on machines but on alienation, on the externalization of feeling. Every type of music and song can become *hardcore* sonority as long as it is perceived in conjunction with the movement that leads man outside himself. Music, after all, is the sound generated from the movement of attraction of bodies become things.

16

Hegel and the Thing as 'also'

According to Schelling what holds together the inorganic world is magnetic cohesion. For Hegel, instead, magnetism is a fiction that hinders the genuine experience of the thing. It is the place of a contradiction. On the one hand, the thing shows itself as a simple unity, a point, on the other hand, it is a collection of elements and determinations different and independent from one another, which maintain among themselves a relation of complete indifference. The punctuality of the thing is dissolved in a multiplicity of separate elements that are added without intimately connecting to one another. The ontological status of the thing can be defined as a being 'also'. Within it, there is always room for some other determination which does not mingle with the others, but does not oppose them either. Therefore Hegel claims that the inorganic world presents an essential porosity, a kind of radical vacuity that offers itself to infinite penetration.

If in Schelling's music theory the sex appeal of the inorganic is connected to magnetic attraction, in Hegel it emerges out of the interpenetration of elements. It is as if making space, giving oneself to the other's penetration, and, at the same time, offering oneself to penetrate the interstices that constantly open up, were inherent to its being thing. A porous world is a multiplicity of openings. In it whoever penetrates is in his turn penetrated, without establishing between them a relation of mutual belonging. Despite infinite and mutual penetrations, the link that connects those who penetrate to those who are penetrated remains superficial, the connection remains extrinsic. The elements, says Hegel, interpenetrate one another, but they do not affect each other.[7] The inorganic world is an inessential existence that has as its basis its own nullity. Nothing succeeds in ever having a form, a limit, a shape endowed with clear margins. The thing is a formless aggregate that receives indiscriminately because it remains indifferent with respect to the permanence of what it receives. In a porous universe one enters, one stays and one leaves, without entailing substantial transformations. However, it seems to me that in the experience of porosity the accent is placed on access, on insertion, on the addition of always new elements, in a word, on the 'also'. The vastness of this addition is in conformity to the infinite excitement of the sex appeal of the inorganic. In the neutral sexuality of the thing that feels the experience of an accessibility to receive and to be received limit-lessly is decisive, almost as if bodies were nothing but pores, cavities, holes, and that in all the smooth and solid parts pores would open into which one could insert oneself and allow inser-tion, almost as if all determinations, figures and forms became undone, opening up craters and chasms.

To be sure, Hegel's notion of thing carries a negative prejudice. Hegel underlines above all what is lacking, the flaw, the deficiency of the status of the thing. It is only starting from the moment when the thing is thought as sentient that one is struck by the indifference, the coldness, the absence of participation and aura that characterizes a relation between two sentient things. But even remaining within the framework outlined by Hegel, are we sure that we can speak of the thing in the plural? If things can be divided and separated to infinity, because their union is extrinsic, it should be equally possible to reassemble them and rejoin them to infinity until they form a single thing. In fact, things fall in a single continuity. Therefore, sometimes, we have the impression that the encounter between two sentient things does not succeed in having a determinate and stable form, and that it proceeds by successive additions. My lover is also my wife, also my slut, also my slave, also my master, also my daughter, also my mother, also my sister, and so on. Proceeding by extension, and not by exclusion, my relation always encroaches on something else. Similarly a porous thought does not remain within safe method-ological limits and always becomes something else. It is also literature, also social theory, also history of ideas, also sexology, also philosophy.

The thing is essentially different from the fragment. The latter has a claim to an autonomous organic unity. It is born spontaneously from within and is posited as an intrinsic self-sufficient unity, a vital principle opposed to the inert and inorganic part. The fragment is the product of Romantic organicist vitalism. It is a very powerful device of exclusion with respect to everything which it reproaches for not being touched by the primordial energy of life. It is not an accident that it was compared by the Romantics to a porcupine whose spines keep it completely separate from the surrounding world and closed within itself. That is why the sex appeal of the inorganic has nothing to do with Romantic love that turns on itself in a self-reflexive spiral and that brings satisfaction in the fulness of its self-sufficiency and its self-overcoming. Beneath the neutral sexuality of the thing that feels always lies a void, a cavity, an opening that asks to be penetrated and possessed, while a Romantic soul is nicely closed within itself as a balloon or as a cartouche, that is as that oval ring that within ancient Egyptian writing enclosed the hieroglyphic name of Pharaoh. An existence which recognizes itself in being thing is internally empty, essentially cavity, cave, crypt. The fragmentary and the porous are opposites of one another. The former is experience of the infinite activity of the autonomous and independent I, the latter is not sufficient unto itself and asks to be filled by attention, care and the help of others. A porous being has its own nullity as ground. As Hegel says, it has its own essence in another, it is in itself insofar as it is for the other.

Walter Benjamin and Ernst Bloch thought of porosity as an essential aspect of the city of Naples and, more generally, of Italy. In their view, the way of being Italian is the negation of form, margin, lines traced with clarity and rigour. Nothing is ever thought of as definitive and conclusive. There is always the possibility of an addition, a complement, a surplus. In architecture as in daily life, there is constantly the experience of transit, interpenetration, without ever determining exactly the demarcation between inside and outside, private and public, day and night, wakefulness and sleep. The way of being Italian would be anti-dialectic, par excellence, precisely for the incapacity or, better, the reluctance, the radical aversion to appointing or maintaining opposites, or even fixing an identity. Porosity is, after all, the result of negation, of 'not this', that Hegel considers to be the first characteristic of being thing. Determinations interpenetrate and the result is a nebula in which they are affirmed and denied simultaneously. This mode of being is apparent, according to Bloch, in Italian art whose basic imprint remains Moorish and Baroque. To be sure, Italian difference seems to be distant either from philosophical attitude, which cannot do without the rigour of the concept, or from sexual disposition, which cannot do without excessive commitment. In what Bloch calls the Italian '*omnia ubique* [everything everywhere]',[8] there is the risk that everything vanishes in a formless mixture without tension, in a lifestyle marked by caution and circumspection, in a miserly and distrustful minimalism. But beginning from the time when in the status of the thing one catches a disturbing and enigmatic greatness that makes possible the comprehension of so many aspects of contemporary society, the Italian difference should be inserted in a much wider context that goes beyond provincial eccentricities, ethnic particularism and cultural specifics. If in Italy one has always been blinded by the splendour of the 'also' and from the infinite penetrations made possible by porosity, perhaps this excessive attention with respect to the inorganic is based on more general and more radical philosophical and sexual premises that go back to antiquity.

It is a fact that Italian culture, ever since ancient Rome, was permeated by a philosophical tendency extraneous and hostile to Platonic ethical and aesthetic organicism, by Stoicism, where the notion of porosity plays a decisive role. In fact, the Stoics think that reality is essentially porous, that a body can pass through another body while occupying the same place, that the world is kept together by a material breath that crosses it in its entirety. However, unlike Hegel, they claim that porosity does not imply at all the existence of the void. The full penetrates and receives whatever turns up, not having any empty spaces within itself. While Hegel's theory of porosity is articulated on a dualism and on the opposition between the inorganic, viewed as empty and inert, and the organic, as living force, Stoic thinking is of an essentially monistic inspiration that leads it to assert, in the most peremptory way, the unity of the real. Therefore, the idea of porosity does not refer to the establishment of the absence of something of which one feels the lack; on the contrary, it guarantees the consistency, solidity and continuity of the real. The fact that it is difficult to represent formally the interpenetration of things does not matter because for the Stoics what constitutes a body is not its visibility, its form, rather its tactility, the fact of being touched and embraced. The Greek word *haptō*, meaning to touch, in Homeric language means to tie a knot, unite, sew together, and, therefore, entails the existence of a more intrinsic link than a simple contact of surfaces. Therefore, when we say that reality is tactile and porous we understand that it is held together by links, knots, joints, and not that it is epidermic, or devoid of content. In fact, the Stoics differentiated mixture both from juxtaposition, where things are held together thanks to an extrinsic link, and from fusion, where things lose their properties completely. In Hegelian terms, the mixture of the Stoics is neither organic nor inorganic. It points to a state in which things are interpenetrated but still preserve their nature. Thus, Stoic thinking goes beyond the dualism between life and non-life, whole and part. Stoics thought that there are no last parts of a division, and that a man is not made up of a greater number of parts than a finger has. Since the cosmos is already strictly connected with itself, strictly speaking, it does not seem possible to add new links, or effect a new penetration, because everything is already connected and interpenetrated.

Philosophy and sexuality, therefore, appear as a type of superfetation because the world is already at its philosophical and sexual maximum. They are at best an assent to what is already there. It is unthinkable that a fragment can detach from the whole and constitute itself autonomously as something separate and self-sufficient, endowed with its proper and essential form. There is only one thing that feels and this is the universe. It is tactile and porous and we can only confirm through philosophy and sexuality its being strictly connected and interpenetrated. Under this aspect, the thinking of the thing and neutral sexuality are a kind of 'also', an addition, a supplement, but neither an alternative nor an extra.

17

Vampirism and Sex Appeal
of the Inorganic

Porosity is the specific characteristic of the vampire, this disturbing figure that had such great success in fantastic literature and the cinema of the nineteenth and twentieth centuries. The principal action of the vampire is precisely that of absorbing, sucking and drinking the blood of its victims, by appropriating their vital lymph as a sponge, and transmitting his mode of being to them. But what is a vampire? What is his sensitive horizon? Those who give and receive the disquieting piercing kiss, what are they trying to prove?

The vampire is a being halfway between life and death. This intermediary situation can be seen as belonging to a dead man who is not completely dead, or to a living being who is not completely living because he is already deprived of some essential aspects of life. The Romanian word *nosferatu*, which means 'not dead', becomes synonymous of vampire, and shows that the vampire must not be seen so much as a real dead that comes back to life, as false dead or, which is the same, false living, or, more essentially, as something else, something different with respect to life and death. This state which is not life or death is precisely the sex appeal of the inorganic, the neutral and impersonal experience of the thing that feels. Now collective imagination, from Romantic *noir* to horror, has been literally obsessed with a non-subjective feeling, not referable to an identity, personal, catalectic and lethargic, anonymous and opaque, inorganic, post-vital, posthuman, pre-mortuary, and pre-funerary.

In the work of Edgar Allan Poe, the great explorer of the boundaries between life and death, the attention to the problem of what one feels when accessing an extreme experience, which goes beyond the normal state of consciousness, returns in an obsessive way. In fact, his characters have for the most part survived terrible events, have escaped enormous dangers against any reasonable expectation. They no longer have anything to fear because they have already known all that is terrible. There are those who have been buried alive, have endured incredible storms, have undergone terrible tortures, have witnessed incredible transformations of their or others' bodies. What all these survivors have in common is their access to another world which, without being an afterworld and transcendental, is certainly radically different from everyday life because it entails the dissolution of subjective identity, the entrance into a kind of monomania of unknown character, the fixation on some phenomenon or on some secondary object that acquires an excessive prominence and importance, and requires absolute and ceaseless attention. Already in Poe the essential is not fear, horror, terror, but what comes after these sentiments. Terror and anguish are only transitory moments that open up for us unexpected horizons. Even in the grave not all is lost. What counts is the after-fear, the after-suffering. Beyond fear and pain, there is a kind of standstill, a suspension of subjective feeling, one enters a kind of lethargy, catalexis, in which the experience of the world becomes vague and opaque. It is as if we did not feel in the first person but only in that indeterminable and porous thing that we have become.

For academic aesthetics, Kant for example, the experience of fear before a dreadful power that threatens our safety, makes it possible to access the sentiment of the sublime which is based on the awareness of the primacy of our spiritual substance. For neutral aesthetics, of which Poe is one of the first and most important theorists, the experience of horror in the face of our subjective identity introduces us into the dimension of the grotesque, where the difference between men and things, the organic and inorganic world, living and non-living, ceases to exist. While academic aesthetics, in its historical development that spans over two centuries from Baumgarten to Adorno, is based on spiritualistic premises that bring it to consider, surreptitiously, as art only learned and moral productions, neutral aesthetics, which develops underground but parallel to it, is interested in staying in syntony with works that can satisfy both popular and critical taste, and in which what counts, above all, is effect, excitement and excess. While in academic aesthetics philosophy accepts under its wings only a feeling purified of any pathological aspect and sublimated in a pleasure without interest, in neutral aesthetics, by contrast, room is found for all so-called perverse sexuality, that is deviant with respect to supersensible elevation and vitalistic intoxication. Sadism, masochism, fetishism and necrophilia form an impressive picture at which philosophy has so far preferred not to look directly. But starting from the moment in which they can be brought together under a single philosophical principle, under the notion of sentient thing, what qualms still prevent it from espousing the cause of the sex appeal of the inorganic? After all, is not deviant and perverse neutral and impersonal sexuality the feeling from which it has always, or at least ever since Descartes, been secretly excited and driven? Is not there already in Hegel, and even more in Schelling, a theory of an aesthetics of the inorganic, a thinking that recognizes for art the irresistible call towards offering itself as thing that feels and taking things that feel, toward being penetrated in every part and in penetrating porous masses that offer themselves unconditionally?

After all, even in the popular imagination of the nineteenth and twentieth centuries, we can say that the sex appeal of the inorganic remains more or less implicit and hidden in vampirism, where the repulsion from the living dead is far greater than the attraction. The fact is that the figure of the vampire, even though rooted within popular Romanian culture and even in ancient culture, acquires particular importance starting from the early nineteenth century with relation to the vitalist turn that with the birth of biology marks a radical discontinuity between the organic and the inorganic world. In fact, while eighteenth-century thought still considered natural history as a process deprived of solutions of continuity, precisely at the beginning of the twentieth century the notions of life and organic unity became the object of a forceful and exalted consideration that opposed them to what is dead and inorganic. This explains why any relation not exclusively spiritual with the world of the dead is destined to arouse a horror unknown to previous ages. The carnal trade with the dead becomes the greatest imaginable perversion. Vampirism, which is a kind of negative necrophilia, acquired, in this fashion, a great impact on popular imagination, entirely novel and exclusive. In the blood that the vampire sucks from his victims one sees a symbolic representation of life for which the dead seem to be avid. Thus, that co-existence of life and death that had constituted a very important characteristic of baroque culture ceased completely. While the condition of the living dead had been for almost two millennia the mark of the Stoic sage and the Christian saint, in the nineteenth and twentieth centuries it could be thought of only in the mode of being of the vampire. In fact, it seemed that life had everything and death nothing, that the living could only give to the dead and that the dead could only take from the living, that any interference of the world of the dead on that of the living appeared necessarily under the aspect of a plague, an infection, a catastrophe, as we can see in F. W. Murnau's film *Nosferatu*.

However, this does not explain the fascination that vampirism continues to exercise on the imagination. The fact is that, however removed and hidden it may be, the key to vampirism is of a sexual nature, as the religious writers of treatises of the seventeenth century well knew. According to them, men and women who had sexual intercourse with vampires, afterwards found their lovers to be mediocre and incapable. What kind of performance does the vampire offer that cannot be equalled by any other mortal? According to these writers, vampires, even though they were equal to men under every aspect, as they were men and women, as well as occupying different roles and conditions in society, have a body of a different quality. Paraphrasing Robert Musil, one could say that they have a body without quality, a body-thing, in which qualities and forms become suspended and irrelevant in favour of the experience of an extension which is given and taken unconditionally. The vampire drinks, drains and sucks dry the bodies of those with whom he engages sexually. It is as if not only the seed but all the liquids were absorbed in his mouth, generating an anguish full of infinite sweetness and total oblivion. In the fantasy that all our blood is absorbed by his kiss is forcefully urged and imperiously asserted the great call of the inorganic. If the body of our lover were really emptied of its blood, her interior would become a great pocket whose lining is no different from the epidermis. It would finally be fit for unlimited penetration that passed through it entirely and wore it like a glove, of which I would be able to feel both the outside and the inside at the same time. Not just that, but through the thin material of her skin it would be possible for me to feel myself doubly, that is my member that fills her entering through the vagina, the anus or the mouth, and my hand that caresses her from outside. As to my lover, she would be transformed into cloth, felt and shaped simultaneously from both sides, in a thing devoid of inside that feels in its every part. The Capuchin convent in Palermo, which preserves and exhibits to the public thousands of dried-up mummies, offers a very large repertory of human skins that have become dry and smooth as parchment. This result was obtained by placing the corpse in a drying room that purged it of all its humours, cleansed it of all its liquids. This temple of the sex appeal of the inorganic, that has nothing to do with vampirism, offers an example of the results that vampirism could reach, once it were freed of its vitalistic prejudices. Any piece of paper, which rolled in my hand and held in my fist, crackles and squeaks, recalls the dried-up skin of the vampire's kiss, the transformation of the flesh into thing, of the organic into the inorganic, and generates an excitement which is increased by the thought of extending sexuality beyond life and beyond that suppurating and maggoty life that cadaverous decomposition continues after death.

Poe writes: 'And the fever called "Living"/ is conquered at last'.[9] The fever called life is finally defeated, but defeated by what? By the eternal peace of the spirit or by the neutral excitement of the thing that feels? By the abandonment to nirvana or by the challenge of those who extend sexuality to the mineral world? By the reduction to zero of all tensions, or by the maintenance of all magnetism, energy and attraction? For instance, there is in Romanticism a tendency that, in connecting the idea of beauty with that of death, generates a profound passion for what is rotten, sickly, putrid. From it is born the idea of Medusa's beauty, depicted precisely by the splendid face of the Medusa, adorned by vipers, bats, toads, worms and other forms of repulsive life. The fascination with corruption that operates in this form of necrophilia is very distant and even opposed to the sex appeal of the inorganic. In fact, in the end, it ·is a development of vitalism beyond the confines of human life, and not the passing to another sensitivity, which emerges from the world of things. As long as we speak of beauty, we are within the sphere of form. However eccentric and bizarre Romantic and decadent taste is, it is not able to make the shift that introduces it to the indeterminable porosity of the thing that feels, and, maybe, not even to the mortified consumption of those who are vampirized. There is in the beauty of disease, death and decomposition not only something vital but something too vital, as in the horrible screams of the dying that do not want to die. That is why sexual orgasm has been compared to a little death, as it is at the service of the life drive and its ruinous race. Instead, vampires, as is well-known, do not die. To suppress them one has to pierce their heart with a stake, performing an operation that evokes and repeats somehow the penetration by their teeth of the throats of their victims.

That is why vampirism is closer to the sex appeal of the inorganic than Medusa's necrophilia. Werner Herzog's *Nosferatu, Phantom of the Night* reveals a disposition to understand the point of view of the vampire which had been left too concealed in previous works on vampires. More psychologically attentive to the motives of vampires are the novels and films that have as protagonist Dracula, whose prototype is the novel by Bram Stoker published at the end of the nineteenth century.

The overcoming of vitalism implicit in the vampire tradition is much more recent and can be characterized by the shift from the horror genre to so-called *splatter punk*, a label which identifies, from 1968 on, narrative and cinematic productions characterized by extreme violence. The identification with the point of view of the murderer, which it proposes, leads to a consideration of bodies as objects, and for this reason does not yet mark the entrance into the neutral and impersonal world of the thing that feels. However, worthy of attention is the fetishism of blood to which it introduces us, allowing us to rethink, in an inorganic and non-vital–spiritualistic key, vampirism and necrophilia.

18

Plastic Landscapes

To travel, cross, transit, run through, explore, penetrate. Contemporary experience of space is formed on a dynamic model that throws the model outside itself into the territory of neutral sexuality. This model transforms it into a thing that feels, which can be added indifferently to the context in which it moves or from which it withdraws. Thus, all conceptions of space that place emphasis on living, dwelling, residing and that think of architecture with reference to the experience of the interior, in more or less dialectical relation to the exterior, are subverted and put aside. Even within this framework the inorganic character of a way of being imposes and asserts itself by force, putting into ridicule and into sentimentalism all good intentions concerning an architectural organization of life that harmonizes form and function, nature and culture, country and city. The organicism that was rampant in reflections on architecture up to the sixties was more or less a humanistic vitalism embroiled in pseudo oppositions between rational and irrational, geometry and curved line, composition and spontaneity.

Much more lucidly, Schelling at the beginning of the nineteenth century thought of architecture as inorganic art, a kind of hardened, petrified, concrete music, and he grouped it together with bas-relief and sculpture under the common heading of the plastic. Now the thesis that architecture is part of the plastic arts makes it, at first sight, the product of the activity of an artisan who shapes, moulds, fashions matter to obtain a shape, but also makes one think that this shape is not definitive, stable, perfect, that is it introduces a temporary element, contingent, if not arbitrary. If architecture is plastic it means that its forms cannot at all be compared to intelligible forms, almost as eternal and immutable as Platonic ideas, but rather to folds, impressions, curvatures. It is not an accident that Schelling compares architecture to tailoring and asks why tailors are not considered the equals of architects. Although he values the latter more than the former, he claims nonetheless that a considerable part of plastic is represented by drapery and clothing, which can be considered the most perfect and most beautiful architecture. The definition of architecture as the plastic of the inorganic, to look closely, does not exalt but mitigates and reduces the importance of the artist understood as subject creator by comparing him to the craftsman. But above all it focuses our attention on the work of architecture understood as physical formation not essentially different from the corneous covering of some species of animals, such as the shells of molluscs or the carapaces of crabs, or from the geological configuration of the earth's crust. In short, architecture exists before construction, before that human activity that builds, constructs, erects independently of need and any utilitarian purpose. We could almost say that human architecture represents the rising to power of something that is already given apart from man. Let it be understood, not because it is ordained by fixed immutable laws but because it is modelled on the bases of events that we cannot define in any other way than sexual. In fact, Schelling claims that in most animal species the artistic instinct is manifested equally as sexual instinct.

Separating architecture from construction can appear odd at first because one usually thinks that architecture is something one adds to construction, as its refinement and embellishment, a kind of surplus, a non-essential addition. Even more odd is to connect it to sexuality, as if to go in and out of a building, to walk in a city, to go through a territory were sexual acts or metaphors of sexual acts. And yet it is precisely construction that desexualizes architecture because it hinders the experience that leads outside itself, focuses attention on the monumentality of the work, abolishes the transit, the flow, the shift through space. Architectural experience is a drifting, an uncontrollable dragging through which the continuous change of perceptive framework changes continuously what can be seen. It does not have a frame or, better, it has a frame that extends to all sides. By definition, it is incomplete but not fragmentary because it makes possible, on the contrary, an experiment with the continuity of space, the mixture and intersection of all things among themselves, the porosity and tactility of the real. It views surfaces and outlines as if they belonged to a body, and finds itself immersed in the penetration of a space which is without solution of continuity, entirely consecutive and without voids. The architectural poetics of Expressionism was perfectly aware of architecture's sexuality when it compared the walls of a house to the epidermis of the human body, but this comparison is driven by an organic and natural perspective that compares architectural production to the symbolic meaning of shells and stalactites. Here, instead, it is a question of an inorganic and artificial sexuality that goes well beyond the symbolism of the phallic columns, obelisks and caves. In the ancient legends of caryatids and telamons, men and women walled alive and transformed into support structures for buildings, there is a mixture of sensitivity and architecture that is close to the sex appeal of the inorganic, as in the myth of Amphion, so dear to Schelling, who with his music persuades stones to come together and give rise to the city of Thebes. But all these comparisons and stories, even though recognizing in architecture a strong sexual value, confuse it with construction, while what we want to place in evidence is a proto-sexuality essential to architecture which exists before and independently of construction.

If cohesion is essential to music, architecture, according to Schelling, is rather characterized by allegory, more specifically, the allegory of the organic in the inorganic. From this suggestive definition we can deduce that in architectural experience is inherent the reference to the other, almost as if the essence of architecture were identifiable only in the dynamism of shifting and transiting. Inorganic sexuality is a crossing of spaces that are contiguous to one another but not equal. Our tireless exploration is directed by a continuous and unstoppable movement that proceeds without jumps or breaks. Architecture can only refer to the organic world of residing, dwelling and living as something, however, which is extraneous and contrary to it. The *genius loci,* the rootedness, the attachment to the earth that constitute the characteristic par excellence of the vegetable world can indeed be the model of architecture, as is evident in Gothic and Indian art, but not in the sense that architecture really shares in this mode of being. Only by allegory and by allusion the columns are trunks and the cities are forests. The meaning of Schelling's comparison between vegetable world and architecture is precisely the opposite of the theories of ethnic organicity. Making us see a house as if it were a plant, or a town as if it were a wood increases our extraneity with respect to the enclosed space of the home and the urban area and establishes the premise of a vision of the world in which men, plants and buildings are united in being things, inorganic entities that nonetheless feel and are endowed with immediate reactive ability. Winckelman is responsible for the comparison, later taken up by Schelling, between the human body and the landscape. The comparison shows clearly, on the one hand, the essential sexuality of architecture as something independent of construction, and on the other, the neutral, impersonal and almost cosmic character of the sexual drifting across territories, mountains and cavities of the human body. To agree with Schelling, the fact that a single body could become a reduced image of the earth and the universe, this is the great horizon that the sex appeal of the inorganic opens up for us. May destiny allow us to travel in it till the hour of our death.

The fundamental confirmation of the inorganic orientation of architectural experience comes precisely from the works and the poetics of the more innovative architects working since the second half of the sixties. The rejection of functionalism, the critical revision of the fundamentals of architecture, the often indeterminate, porous aspect of interiors of buildings that lack any clear delimitation, the privileging of a public building topology destined for transit, performances, cultural tourism, the dissolution of housing units, attention to spaces of transit rather than residences, are similar aspects of a tendency oriented toward the abandonment of any organic character. The deconstructive movement that in the eighties acquired great importance internationally must not be understood negatively as the end of architecture, if anything just the opposite, as the separation of architecture from construction, as the claim of its autonomy with respect to building, as the expansion of plastic space beyond the limits of property, as the extension of architectural competence to ever wider contexts, as the commitment to an invention of the landscape on an always greater scale. And here architecture clashes with that petty planning and administration of the existing that no longer needs architecture, but construction alone, and that represents the real destruction of any plastic experience. But at the same time, architecture meets philosophy, to which one owes the introduction of the term deconstruction in cultural debate. Now philosophical deconstruction is not so much a type of negative dialectic in which the opposites confront each other, giving way to paradoxes which are impossible to resolve. Neither is it a schizophrenic logic that undoes the building of metaphysics, generating infinite ruins to be put back together arbitrarily. In a more essential way, deconstruction is the emancipation of philosophy from construction, that is from that role of foundation and legitimization of the social organism that it has played for centuries, if not millennia. To construct we no longer need philosophy, just as to build we no longer need architecture. Philosophy and architecture are finally autonomous, since their services are no longer required. Finally they can get involved in inorganic experiences that link them to something even more important and vast than the mediation and administration of economic factors. Deconstruction is neither the end nor the fragmentation of architecture and philosophy. On the contrary, it represents the extension of plastic experience to everything visible, the extension of conceptual experience to everything existing. It marks the triumph of architecture and philosophy, the restoration of a relation of direct contact between these and all those aspects of the cultural and scientific imaginary that one meets in the paradigm of the sentient thing, in the sex appeal of the inorganic.

In deconstruction is implicit an architectural and philosophical maximalism which is solidly anchored in the neutral, impersonal and suspended character of experience. It puts into motion a device of de-spiritualization and de-vitalization that can be applied to any material. The dissolution of any form and function does not indicate a vandalistic transgression, on the contrary it aims at showing contiguity and continuity existing between entities shown by tradition to be opposites. To construct and to build means positing a violent discontinuity, a discrimination, a hiatus between what is culture and what is nature, what is rational and irrational. But everything by now is already architectural, everything is already philosophical. One cannot contain the building or the city within themselves. They cross on all sides in the street, in the landscape. In the same way philosophy can no longer be contained in an academic course or in a school of thought. The philosopher is no longer the master who teaches the ways of wisdom and virtue, but he is an explorer who finds in the present world material for those extreme thoughts that philosophical tradition has already in large part elaborated, by limiting and circumscribing its scope and range to the non-human and non-vital world. To do architecture without constructing and to do philosophy without edifying means transforming them into adventures, travels, where one ventures with the expectation of extending, through the offer of oneself to a neutral and impersonal movement, the sphere of the visible and the thinkable.

The work of architects, the Polish-born Daniel Libeskind and the Iranian Zaha Hadid, is evidence that deconstruction in architecture does not lead to a playful and humorous minimalism but to an extreme plastic experience that dissolves forms and functions, extends beyond every boundary the perception of space and amplifies feeling to planetary and cosmic dimensions. In their work, architecture becomes the design of a world in which the distinctions between technical object and living body, inorganic nature and urban conglomeration are abolished. It seems that the whole planet is covered by a garment of which the mountains as well as the cities, the oceans as well as the industrial plants, are only the folds, the gorges, the outcrop. One moves from one to the other through a transit, a movement that goes from the same to the same. The configurations taken on by the earthly mantle seem temporary and devoid of foundation, almost as if the entire universe, as the ancient Stoic philosophers imagined, was destined to be destroyed in order to return to being the same as before. In the simultaneous affirmation of the transitoriness and perpetuity of plastic configurations lies the most profound insight of deconstructive architecture, which escapes both vitalistic organicism and utilitarian functionalism.

Architecture turns its attention to landscape which asserts itself as the true protagonist of spatial experience. Unlike spectacle which implies the existence of an eye is looking at it, the notion of landscape derives from its geographical origins an impersonal nature that departs completely from the subjective point of view. The neutral sexuality of plastic experience can be described as a dislocation of feeling in a geotypical context. It is no longer man who feels the landscape because now he is himself part of it. This insertion of human life into the landscape, however, must not be understood as the objectifying premise typical of the scientific approach of classical and systematic geography, which ignores the 'lived' dimension of spatial experience. The fact that man is placed inside and not outside the landscape is a given that emerges first from daily life then from architecture. People, by now, no longer belong to themselves but to the place where they move, they are mobile elements of environments to which they can be added or removed without the whole being substantially altered. To architecture also belong human bodies at the same level as houses, forests and mountains. The director Gottfried Reggio has been the genial interpreter of this assimilation of everything extant to landscape, in his two films *Koaanisquatsi* and *Powaqqatsi*, which constitute a grandiose epic of the inorganic. The first, whose title in Hopi alludes to a condition of life which is unbalanced and disintegrating, shows the continuity between the inorganic life of deserts, volcanoes, clouds and the industrial metropolitan world. The second, whose title, also in Hopi, alludes to a parasitical entity that feeds on others' lives, is entirely devoted to underdeveloped countries. In it, the human body, singularly and collectively represented, acquires an architectural value. It is seen as the element of a plastic landscape that does not differentiate at all from inanimate or mechanical nature. The enigmatic character of these two films makes it possible to read them as a vehement and almost apocalyptic protest against the devitalization of the world, and as a splendid illustration of a condition that succeeds in turning into architecture even and especially the uninhabitable.

Plastic landscape already implies, after all, an estrangement of feeling, because feeling is alienated, displaced and dehumanized. It has acquired a complete autonomy with respect to man. This new condition is best interpreted by the techno-morphism of the Japanese Shin Takamatsu, in whose work the boundaries between the human body and the world seem to be suppressed, not because they both partake of a great universal life but because the task of perceiving is assigned to technology, which represents an extension of the human senses. Thus, an inorganic feeling is asserted to which man has access indirectly because it comes from outside his body and not from inside. Up to now, from the outside came only the perceived not the perceiving, the heard not the sentient. Now, instead, man can perceive because he has adjusted to being himself a sentient thing similar to electronic sensors. Architecture can no longer be the metaphor of the human body, following the organicist model, because the body is already architecture, even in its innermost and secluded parts. For instance, by means of intestinal endoscopy one can see live the insides of one's own abdomen. It offers a plastic landscape, a view of which I access through technology. It is not I who see myself directly, but it is the camera which sees for me. My body becomes extraneous to me not only objectively but also subjectively. In fact this opposition between objective and subjective is dissolved. What counts is the neutral experience of self-penetration. As if a neutral entity, a thing, were excited by a penetration that sees what it penetrates. Imagine that your penis, equipped with a camera, penetrates the cave-like landscape of the vagina and that through technological instrumentation it were possible to receive in the brain all the sensations that you would feel in a normal intercourse. This is the sex appeal of the inorganic, because the penis does not belong to you any more than does the vagina you are penetrating. It is also the element of an architectural landscape that generates a quite different excitement to the natural one. It does not rush toward an orgasm, but explores, crosses, transits. The difference between natural and artificial is overcome in favour of a sentient landscape rich with indentations, recesses and protuberances that feels in your place and constitutes an allegory of the entire world. In fact the vaginal landscape and the cosmic landscape are each allegories of the other. Between the two there is no supremacy. Excitement is born and is maintained indefinitely through sliding, shifting from one to the other. If a vagina were only a vagina and not an allegory of the earth's landscape, the excitement could not be unlimited. Thus, if the earth's landscape referred only to itself, architecture would only be a construction and a representation of the territory. One goes from the vagina to the cosmos and from the cosmos to the vagina as in a transit that goes from the same to the same, because neither the vagina nor the world, and not even our body, are any longer places where one can live.

Computerized design allows entrance to a new dimension that radicalizes contemporary architectural experience. Described first in science fiction novels, it is called *cyberspace*. As a completely spatialized visualization of information, cyberspace transforms everything into landscape and introduces into it an extraordinary and astonishing dynamism. The key characteristics of contemporary architectural research, from the abandonment of any constructional bias to transit, from spatial continuity to inorganicity, find unlimited development and intensification. Cyberspace is the practical realization of Schelling's idea according to which architecture is spatialized music. However, it must not be understood as a dematerialization or, worse, a spiritualization of reality. What is important is the dissolution of the formal into the sentient, almost as if the landscape were to melt by acquiring an autonomous capacity to palpitate and pulsate. That is why it has been said that cyberspace creates a liquid architecture. In the measure that the user is transformed into a cybernaut who navigates in virtual reality, he learns to perceive his own real body as a sentient thing not essentially different from the almost sentient landscapes of electronic architectures.

19

Hegel and the Thing 'all of one piece'

After indetermination and porosity, for Hegel the third characteristic of the inorganic emerges from the fact that the thing does not have an interior distinguishable from an exterior but is, so to speak, the outside in itself, in general. Essence and phenomenon, reality and appearance, interiority and exteriority are not distinguishable one from the other. In essence there is nothing which is apparent and the phenomenon does not show anything different from what essence contains. Thus, Hegel quotes a phrase from Goethe according to whom nature has neither stone nor peel but is 'all of one piece'.[10] Precisely from this experience of radical exteriority, which abolishes the distinction between inside and outside, moves the sex appeal of the inorganic. Giving oneself as a sentient thing and taking a sentient thing exercise an irresistible attraction because they exclude any reference either to a secret interiority different from what it appears, as well as to an exterior that alters what is inside, because they finally place themselves on this side of truth and falsehood, because they hand us over, irremediably and inexorably, to a wide open and unfolding exteriority, which arrives in all the most remote recesses of our being.

What entails feeling as a thing all of one piece, we can understand from the way in which Hegel thinks of its opposite, that is, life, self-consciousness, being for itself. Now the living is a relatively closed system, self-finalized, endowed with an inside different from an outside, whose essential character is desirability. Unlike the thing which is porous, the living being is a multiple constituted of limbs that essentially belong to him. Since the primary goal of the living is preservation, it is pervaded by an endless restlessness and is marked by infinite mutability.

Finally, while the becoming of the inorganic is a transit, a passing from the same to the same, the becoming of the living is a process, a movement qualified by temporal irreversibility.

Hegel attributes to the living three characteristics: sensibility, irritability and reproduction. Sensibility is the pure vibration of the body understood in its inseparability from the soul. Here the body is understood precisely as a living entity which has its essential unity. However important is its receptivity, it is always reflected on the inside, so that the determinate sentiment that the living has of himself constitutes the fundamental aspect of his feeling. The feeling of the thing is somewhat different since it does not belong to it essentially. The thing cannot receive and keep something within itself that comes from outside, because as we said, it is all of one piece, so that its feeling is devoid of reflection in something more intimate. To the subjective and self-conscious feeling of the living, is opposed the neutral and impersonal feeling of the thing. The latter is characterized by a suspension, an *epochē*, a hesitation that prevents it from acquiring that liveliness and that self-reflecting presence typical of subjective self-consciousness. To read in the glassy and opaque look of your lover who is sucking your member the physical and unfolding demonstration of a detachment from passions, as advocated by the ancient Sceptics and Stoics, constitutes an experience from which it is almost impossible to separate oneself. Neutral and impersonal sexuality has nothing to do with the confusing process of subjective life which, in the grip of appetite, greed and desire, runs tumultuously and plunges in an infinite and anxious restlessness.

The second aspect of living for Hegel is irritability. It is an allergic relation, an exaggerated reaction to the environment with which it constantly struggles to maintain itself. Its survival depends on the subjugation of the inorganic world. To life, therefore, inheres a polemical and aggressive disposition that leads it to identify sexuality with power. On the contrary, neutral sexuality stands on the tendency to establish and maintain states of equilibrium. These conditions of stability are not immovable, but constitute the result of ceaseless relations of feedback, retro-action, and self-regulation. Instead of struggles for life and death there are dynamic equilibria among infinite interactive entities that unceasingly correct the deviations that could bring the entire system to collapse. Even in this case, it is the ancient Stoic idea of tone, understood as a dynamic principle of the cohesion of the cosmos, which constitutes the theoretical antecedent of the sex appeal of the inorganic. Victory is no longer viewed as an overcoming but as a process of adjustment, giving one's consent to something that provides us with a much richer and more intense experience than that resulting from self-consciousness.

The third aspect of living for Hegel is reproduction. With it life becomes something concrete that establishes a relation between a subject and another subject of its kind. In other words, it implies the difference between the sexes. Natural sexuality, which for Hegel constitutes the vital process, introduces in the subject an absolute contradiction. It is marked by the need, the contrast with an objective exteriority which constitutes, however, an essential aspect of its determining. The subject is as if it were split in two and from this disassociation pain is born, which Hegel defines as the privilege of living beings. There is something that tears you apart in natural sexuality. It stems from the fact that exteriority which excites, touches and penetrates the subject does not remain external, but is already in itself and for itself in him. As does Kant, Hegel gives a vision of sexual experience which is not at all idyllic or toned down. He does not hide the violence of the subject on something external, which constitutes anyway a double of himself. To be sure, this exteriority turns into interiority, is elevated to universality, constitutes the genre, becomes procreation of a new individual, but precisely in this overcoming it ceases to be sexuality. However, desire, greed, lust which qualify life are inseparable from an excruciating contradiction. The living being that constitutes the double of the subject is still always another independent individual. Certainly, this contradiction can be lived without pain and with detachment, laughing instead of crying. But humour, which in Western tradition is so closely related to the obscene, does it not always originate in the experience of a conflict? The very essence of natural and organic sexuality, which cannot escape being tragic or comic, is ignored by the beautiful souls of sexual liberation and recreational sex.

In the world of things that feel, reproduction is separate from generation. It can be thought of rather as repetition, genetic engineering, cloning. Above all the link with sexuality, which finally becomes autonomous, is undone. In the sex appeal of the inorganic there is no suffering, or subject, or reflection, or interiority and exteriority. It is all of one piece, does not know hiatus between the inorganic world and life, is not moved by desire, by lust that comes from interiority. Neutral sex, as the sperm for the ancient Stoics, seems to be something that really does not belong to man. It is not an instrument of which he can dispose of as he likes, but a way of feeling that is imposed on him with absoluteness, that he cannot escape, dominate or plead for. The wide-open accessibility and all of one piece of the sex appeal of the inorganic is not an accessibility that the subject can dispose of as he likes. One gains access to it through a long road where all subjective affections are abolished or at least suspended.

20

Desire and Sex Appeal of the Inorganic

The call to neutral and impersonal sexuality can be understood only when all desires are satisfied. The sex appeal of the inorganic, in fact, is a sexuality without desire that we can begin to feel only from the moment when the obstacles that prevent subjective affections have been eliminated. In fact, the latter with their spiritual longings and organic desires bar the journey to the infinite path of the thing that feels. If my mind and my eyes are full of images of the thing I desire, if the forms of my body fill the mind and eyes of the person who desires me, we remain in an emotional tonality characterized by lack, absence, deprivation which is just the opposite of the unlimited availability that the world of things opens up for us.

Desire is connected now with seeing, now with doing, now with contemplation, now with action. What it lacks is precisely feeling because in this desire it is satisfied and vanishes. If with it sexuality also vanishes, it means that we did not go beyond the organic world, the kingdom of life, subjective self-consciousness, which rushes forward from goal to goal, always dominated by worry and anxiety. Sexology is so strictly connected to an organic vision of sex that it does not even have a word to designate a sexuality without desire. Paradoxically what comes closer to it are the phenomena characterized by excess of desire such as nymphomania and satyriasis that Krafft-Ebing, the famous writer of treatises on perversions, includes under the category of sexual hyperaesthesia, abnormal and morbid sexual excitability. But while nymphomania or satyriasis are connected rather with the difficulty or the impossibility of satisfying desire, and therefore lead to a condition of frustration and checkmate, inorganic

sexuality is similar to a satisfied excitement and implies a reciprocity, a community of feeling among the partners engaged in
it, and even a kind of intellectual enthusiasm, cerebral erethism,
conceptual extremism that derive from philosophy. To be sure,
sexology knows a whole series of direct practices to delay orgasm
indefinitely. Here, however, it is not a question of techniques
aiming at deferring desire, but of entrance to another dimension that implies the suspension of desire. Finally, unlike Oriental
eroticism, which employs yoga and Zen to arrive at a state of
spiritual elevation and detachment from the world, the sex appeal
of the inorganic is rather a developing world, abolishing the
distance that separates man from things.

In Western tradition exists a type of spirituality that assigns to
desire a meaning of primary importance. From Plotinus, for
whom thinking is desiring the good, to Lévinas who defines desire
as a relation with the absolutely Other, through the mysticism of
Meister Eckhart for whom desire brings identification with God,
the Flemish Ruisbroek, according to whom desire is the very
basis of prayer, the Spanish Juan de la Cruz who views desire
as the stimulant that provokes the search for unity with God,
is transmitted through the centuries an exaltation full of fervour and zeal for a spirituality for which absence counts more
than possession. In this an apologia of desire merge, on the one
hand, the acknowledgment of the destitution of the human condition, on the other, the assertion of the transcendental character
of desire. Georges Bataille is the thinker who in the twentieth
century worked out the transposition of this sensibility from the
spiritual to the sexual level. Thanks to him, sexuality and philosophy have been finally united in erotic excess. This union, however, occurred under the sign of the negative and transgression.
The experience to which it leads is that of torment, torture and
martyrdom. Therefore, Bataille's eroticism shifts from a spiritualistic sensualism and a deadly vitalism, and only sometimes does
it arrive at the inorganic.

The sex appeal of the inorganic is inspired by a type of feeling
opposite to the desiring mysticism and it is inscribed in a tradition that privileges presence with respect to absence, availability
with respect to lack. Possession does not mean wealth. In fact, one

can have almost nothing at one's disposal, as in the case of the ancient Cynics who inaugurated this way of being. Abundance does not come from the objective quantity of things which one possesses, but from the fact that one does not desire anything, one is contented with what one has. Entering into the territory of neutral sexuality, one can take away fairly quickly all the organic desires connected with orgasm, ejaculation, figures and forms, but nothing in theory prevents me being with my genitals in a similar relation of exteriority, or my hand being as impersonal as the mouth of my partner, or as an anonymous hand that is offered occasionally.

Stoicism has always been the enemy of desire, par excellence, and can be considered a development and maturing of Cynicism. It shows that the ways to arrive at neutral and suspended sexuality are many, including homosexuality, common possession of women, incest. For Zeno of Citium there is nothing absurd, or abominable, in having sex with your own mother. What is questionable is not the act but desire, the overwhelming drive that pulls you toward non-present goods. It is based on an erroneous judgement that consists in privileging the future over the present. This Stoic negation of desire is at the origin of a way of feeling that views peace of mind and consolation as something obtainable in any state or condition of life. Working underground throughout the centuries, it is above all in the modern era, from the sixteenth to the eighteenth centuries, that it finds the opportunity to develop and express itself completely. The opinion of Ignatius Loyola, according to whom eternal love is even more ready to bestow holiness than we are to desire it, fits in with this tradition whereby what is given, what is available, namely, the present is much more valuable than what is desired, coveted, that is the future. Between the sixteenth century and the seventeenth century, in Flanders, Giusto Lipsio became the bearer of an explicit revival of Stoicism. As is well known, Rubens was deeply influenced by Flemish Neo-Stoicism; his famous painting *The Four Philosophers* represented the climate of suspended and strong feeling that characterizes this experience. In fact, neutral sexuality is not a state of inertia, of reducing excitement to zero, eliminating all tensions, is not Nirvana, or

Freud's death drive, and not even lethargy, that is a state of erection of indeterminate time entirely deprived of sensibility. Quietism, fatalistic and defeatist renunciation, paralysis, are more indirect affirmations of desire than actual suspensions of it. The sex appeal of the inorganic is closer to an existence full of wonder than to the very equal and apathetic life of the Sceptics. In short, we are very far from sexual anaesthesia. The sex appeal of the inorganic is more an after-desire than a without-desire.

The most acute analysis of sexual desire produced by contemporary philosophy, Sartre's *Being and Nothingness*, shows very well the failure of desire founded on a contradiction that it cannot resolve. On the one hand it looks at the body as an organic totality in a living situation, on the other it is up against a flesh that is pure contingency of presence. On the one hand there is the body which is life and spirit, not the mere sum of its elements, but its total form, existence in a situation which has conscience as its horizon; on the other, there is the flesh which is thing, facticity, comparable to a cloak, a garment, a datum without transcendence. On the one hand, there is the look, the double movement of me who looks at you and you who looks at me; on the other, there are the eyes, these little balls that in Bataille's *Histoire de l'oeil* are compared to eggs and testicles. Now, according to Sartre, desire is wanting precisely to appropriate a consciousness become flesh. This claim implies that I reveal myself to the other as flesh and that I have conscience of the fact that the other sees me the same way. In short it is not enough to desire, one has to desire to be desired and to know that one is actually being desired. What is striking in Sartre's analysis is first of all the close connection between desire and seeing, almost as if a sexuality thought of as desire implied necessarily a primacy of sight over the other senses. We have already mentioned that the hegemony of the visual leads to the exaltation of form, organic unity, beauty whose roots are in ancient Greece, and through Neoplatonism makes its way to the societies of popular, integrated, totalitarian spectacle. When we say that neutral sexuality has nothing to do with desire it means that the moment has finally come to emancipate sexuality from beautiful appearance, from the contemplative ecstasy of beautiful young men, beautiful women and beautiful ideas, from that spiritualistic aestheticism that purports to reconcile everything with everything in aspiration toward the transcendent. Sight is one of the senses that grasps the form of the body as an organic unity, but the inorganic is not a form. A cyborg, this new edition of the cynical and stoic Hercules, is neither beautiful nor ugly. It no longer has a body. The technological prostheses constitute an extension of the senses that separate and alienate them from the organic body. The senses by now are independent and autonomous with respect to the organism. Those who still swear by the body generally believe they are the bearers of a radical alternative with respect to spiritualism, in the name of the free blossoming of desires and of their fullest satisfaction. But these poor souls, in their vitalistic stupor, have not yet realized that what is living in the body is precisely the soul, and that desire, however materialistic are its cravings, is by definition a panting, a longing for an unreachable beyond. Instead of confronting the hard actuality of the thing that feels, they run after beautiful shapes and they waste away for a body that by now has exploded in a thousand pieces. To return once again to Bataille, a human eye that glides between the buttocks of such an experienced woman as Simone, who introduces him to her own flesh, has nothing any more to do with looking. That eye is already a mini-camera.

In Sartre's analysis there is a second aspect of desire that is even more important than seeing: incarnation. In fact, desire is making the other incarnate in his eyes as flesh, and at the same time revealing oneself to the other as flesh. Now, precisely because of the fact that an incarnation is necessary, the starting point of desire is spiritual. On the contrary, in neutral sexuality the thing comes first and above all. It is not I who reveal myself as flesh, but it is the thing that I am that shows itself to me as sentient. In Sartre, the contradiction between conscience and flesh is resolved in favour of the first. The checkmate of desire consists precisely in the impossibility of maintaining the tension between existence and carnality. In the sex appeal of the inorganic desire belongs to the past, it no longer exists, because it originates precisely from a flesh which is already autonomous and impersonal, which, therefore, is more a thing than flesh.

To say flesh, for instance, means referring to something perishable, corruptible and temporary, while neutral sexuality brings with it a guarantee of resistence and long duration. An entity deprived of interiority, whose determinations and whose forms are irrelevant, cannot be called either body or flesh. It is neither desirable, nor feels desire, rather, it is prey to an excitement that perpetually is nourished on the thought of giving itself as a thing that feels.

21

Overflowing Installations

If it is relatively easy to consider music and architecture as inorganic arts, it is more difficult to think of a picture or a statue as a thing. In fact, this idea runs counter to the entire aesthetic tradition that sees in the work of art in general, but especially in painting and in sculpture, an entity characterized by an inner organization, similar to that of a living being. At the origin of this aesthetic organicism there is, probably, the preponderant place occupied by the human figure in these arts, but it is significative that it has not been marred by abstractionism. On the contrary, non-figurative art has paradoxically even boosted and emphasized the presumed organic unity of the work of art almost as if it were necessary to the very survival of painting and sculpture to make immediately self-evident the insurmountable distance that separates the artistic product from all other objects. Precisely because paintings and statues are the most material, flexible works and the most intimately connected to the market, they need a spiritualistic and vitalitistic surplus that justifies the fact of having a price much higher than the other handcrafted and industrial commodities.

However, it has been the case for some time now that the sex appeal of the inorganic has secretly infiltrated and installed itself even in painting and sculpture, corroding slowly as woodworm the formalist idealism of images and appearances. This action unfolded substantially in two phases. The first one, which consists in the transformation of the work of art into a unique object, is tied to the problematic of collecting. It is already fully present in the nineteenth century and constitutes, strictly speaking, more of an antecedent of inorganic excitement than a complete manifestation. The second, which dissolves, instead, the unique object in a sentient thing, belongs to our present cultural trend. It is connected to the open horizon of installations and to the great itinerant exhibitions, and to art as the interface of complex cultural transactions.

When we think of the dissolution of the work of art, we imagine it more or less with reference to temporality, as an ageing and deteriorating process of the materials from which it is made. Colours lose their brightness, the support is altered by the light, humidity and other physical factors. From the necessity of remedying the damages of time, originates the problematic of restoration, which generally has no doubts as to the organic unity of the work of art to be repaired. However, there exists a spatial dissolution of the work of art which is less evident but more subtle because it aims at dissolving the very identity of the work. This attempt begins from the moment in which the work is no longer thought of in itself, but with reference to other similar works with which it cooperates in constructing a collection. As long as the work is considered in itself, its aesthetic relevance is centred on the relation that it entertains with the outside world, which can be either that of imitation or innovation, dependency on the real existence of what it represents or emancipation from any practical interest. Instead, when it is placed within a collection, its aesthetic centre shifts toward the relation that it entertains with other works, namely, of affinity as concerns all those aspects that justify its being included in the series, and of dissimilarity, as concerns all those aspects that establish its singularity. The latter acquires sense and importance precisely on the basis of the exercise of a comparison, of a contrast. To make a play on words, we could say that a collection is born from collating, from comparison. The spiritual and organic world is succeeded by the porous and manifold world of unique objects, which are such by virtue of the connection that constitutes them as elements of a logical class to the exclusion of any other. The collection represents an important step toward the sex appeal of the inorganic because it despiritualizes and devitalizes what it collects, but does not represent yet the entrance to a neutral and impersonal territory of the things that feel. The object of a collection no longer has an organic personality, but possesses an identity whose centre of gravity does not fall internally, but externally, in the comparison between it and other pieces. Paradoxically the unique subject is something less physically material than the work. It is as if it were endowed with pseudopods, sensorial protrusions whose value and meaning depend on the relation with objects in the same series. The collector's mentality establishes an objective comparison that displaces the essence of the subject. This no longer has its proper place but is subject to an order, to a location whose criteria are extraneous to it. Naturally this does not exclude at all the most careful considerations of its specific particularities. On the contrary, its uniqueness is established precisely by contrast. The unique object is anomalous by definition and the collection is a gathering of anomalies collected on a certain scale.

The libido of collecting is not yet a neutral sexuality because it is still too cautious and timid. Driven by a desire to accumulate it is not capable of being really a perversion but only an anomaly, a sub-product of the organic. This is clear from idiogamy, the condition of someone excited by a single body, which, therefore, becomes the exclusive object of his desire. Now this curious situation that involves someone sexually with one partner alone seems to be halfway between the spiritual and the inorganic, between the love directed to the person and the neutral sexuality of the sentient thing. In idiogamy, the experience of obliged fidelity is powerful, the fact that the will cannot do anything against an excitement which is set in motion independently of the opposite subjective intention. When someone is faithful, despite the intention of betraying you, simply because he/she does not find a substitute for your body, it is clear that you have become a unique irreplaceable object. What is exciting is not so much the acquisition of such great power, as the sensation that your body has escaped the wear and tear of time, ageing or, better, that its decline does not matter because it is already appreciated today not for its shape but for its singularity and particularity, because it is the subject of a sexual idiogamy, for which a wrinkle or a pound more is irrelevant. Your skin is like the leather of a bound book, your cunt is like the fold in a pillow. They remain that book and that pillow that are unique, even if a little worn and torn. However, the objective singularity of your body does not reside in it. It is born from comparative collecting that has singled it out, precisely, as a unique object. Idiogamy arises out of polygamy. We need to have tried out many bodies to be able to see one as a unique object. For a long time, the bodies with which we unite seem spirits or animals. If we put them all together the result is not yet a collection but a graveyard or a zoo.

A hidden and complex relation links collecting to photography. Even though, at first sight, the technological reproduction of the image is precisely the opposite of the cult that surrounds the unique object, which is part of an ordered collection, both collecting and photography share the same tendency to dissolve the spatial confines of the work. While the unique object stands within a scheme of affinity and diversity that connects it to other pieces, the act of photography constitutes the example par excellence of a practice of radical externalization. In front of a camera lens, nature is really 'all of one piece'. However, this activity remains halfway between organic and inorganic. On the one hand, the framing defines with accuracy the limits of photography, on the other, it includes within itself incongruous elements whose encounter is merely casual. When, as in artistic photography, one proceeds in advance to exclude what seems to be discordant with the coherence of the image, the artificiality of this isolation produces the opposite effect, standardizing the photographed object with everything visible. Whether we are dealing with a portrait, a landscape, an object or an assembly, one always gets the impression that a will of serial proliferation is at work in photographic practice which can be manifested either in shooting the same subject in various poses, or in shooting analogous subjects. Thus, photography never succeeds in getting to the living aura of the work of art, not only because of its technical characteristics that exclude the existence of an original but, more essentially, because in it seems implicit the reference to a multiplicity, a portfolio, within which only the single image can acquire a sense and a place. The acquisition of a photographic eye consists, precisely, in avoiding the naive attitude that privileges exclusively the relation between image and the reality it represents. What counts is the relation between photographs, the sequence, the sliding of the image outside itself. The single photograph, thus, seems the element of a polyptych, the tessera of a mosaic that extends on all sides to infinity. When the contours of the figures do not adhere perfectly, the inorganic effect turns out increased and strengthened. After all, any photograph urges the juxtaposition of imaginary grids that divide it to infinity, emancipating it from the naive realism of representation.

Besides photography, intense experiences of inorganic sexuality are also provided by the cartoon. Here the solicitation toward another image is obligatory because the cartoon implies a temporal development, it is a type of story developed by images. However, the fact that the temporal sequence is at once present and available, printed in a magazine whose order of fruition depends exclusively on the reader, turns the cartoon into a genre which is itself extraneous to organic vitalism. Particularly striking are those designers who, possessed by a kind of *horror vacui*, fill the entire available space with design. In this negation of form and profile is not displayed a tendency toward completeness, rather, a porous sensibility that dissolves the work through unlimited additions. This type of cartoon recalls the horror of the void that characterizes certain ornamental designs or certain psychopathological productions.

Collecting, photography and cartoon anticipate and prepare the dissolution of any organic perspective without however realizing it fully. Henry James's novel, *The Spoils of Poynton*, shows, for example, how a collection can aspire to that organic unity that characterizes the work of art. Photography fosters the pretence of preserving a livid experience. The cartoon, finally, is too dependent on narrative language and on its intention to narrate a life event. It is only with installation that the work is, indeed, transformed in thing, in inorganic non-utilitarian entity, rich in symbolic dimension. With installation, the work overflows out of itself and acquires a radical and extreme exteriority. This expansion does not stop at the area which contains it, since, in general, it has a temporary character and is strictly connected with a specific occasion. The photographs, and eventually the videos, that hand down the memory, are an integral part of it.

Therefore, installations are a kind of happening represented by things rather than by people, events whose protagonists are overflowing and ejaculating entities, digests of information and messages that invade and overwhelm us. Installations must not be considered the object of a visitor's evaluation. The relation with a visitor is completely reversed with respect to the traditional visit to museums and galleries. It is the installation that feels the visitor, welcomes him, touches him, feels him up, stretches out to him, makes him enter into it, penetrates him, possesses him, overwhelms him. One does not go to exhibitions to see and enjoy art, but to be seen and enjoyed by art. Voyeurism belongs to organic, formalistic and natural sexuality. In the inorganic world, instead, it is the sentient things who see us and desire us. We can only offer ourselves to their suspended libido and bear in mind that the greatest inconvenience is certainly not their interest but their indifference.

The top of the sex appeal of the inorganic in the so-called figurative arts, for now, seems to me reached by the American Cindy Sherman whose installations are just photographed. She is the author of photographs that represent sexual manikins in seductive poses, wooden mouths and vaginas that solicit our presence, eyes that penetrate and go through us looking beyond us.

22

Heidegger and the Thing as Reliability

Even though Heidegger never speaks of sexuality in his works, it is only with him that the path of thinking and the sex appeal of the inorganic, which had already crossed for centuries, reveal their essential belonging together. In what way does a thinking which is constantly crossed by a questioning on the essence of Being entertain such a narrow relation with the neutral sexuality of the sentient thing? The fact is that Heidegger looks for Being not in the spirit, as Hegel does, or in life, as Nietzsche does, but precisely in the thing. He places the thing at the centre of his questioning and he turns it into the subject of a suspended meditation, independent of the scope of its usability and objectivity, which plunges us in an emotional tonality unknown to either religious spirituality or empirical psychology. Thinking the thing, thus, is feeling the thing with the exception that this feeling is untouched by a desire or fear of it. In any case, this would not suffice in defining this feeling as sexual. Heidegger's reflection could be seen, as it is most commonly seen, as a kind of ascesis, an exercise in chastity, temperance, abstinence. Now, in my view, ascesis is not at all a synonym of moderation, in fact, it is an excessive and extreme exercise. Heidegger acknowledges an ascesis of sexuality, namely, the access to a non-participating sexuality, suspended and impersonal, other and different with respect to the natural and vitalistic one. But I have not yet replied to the question why a meditation on the thing, which for Heidegger is understood almost as synonymous with *Dasein*, acquires an essentially sexual character. Why does it not remain on a purely aseptic or academically boring cognitive level? What is the

hidden perversion, the displacement, the *détournement* responsible for philosophy's shift from measure to excess, from chastity
to sexuality?

In Heidegger this excess is strictly connected to the essence of
the thing, to thingness (*Dingheit*). First of all we have to state
that the thing is neither an instrument nor a utensil, nor a
means. As long as I remain within the sphere of usability, as long
as I do not allow the thing to rest in its being thing, as long as I
see it in the function of attaining a goal, I have precluded the
possibility of accessing its availability which is more essential,
more complete, more autonomous, and more extensive than any
instrumental use. Our ignorance and our contempt for things is
such that they are generally considered only and exclusively in a
relation of subordination with respect to our subjective will
or to our desires. But, in so doing, we are doing violence to the
thing and we prevent it from showing and giving itself completely to neutral excitement. The discovery of the essence of
things goes hand in hand with the dismissal of any desire and
individual cupidity. Therefore when I give myself as thing, I do
not mean at all to offer myself to the exploitation and the benefit
of others. I do not offer myself to the other but to the impersonal
movement that at the same time displaces the other from himself
and allows him in his turn to give himself as thing and to take
me as thing.

Therefore, we must not confuse the thing with the object
of representation. The thingness of the thing does not reside in
the fact of being an object represented, or in the objectivity
of the object, in its being before and independent of the subject.
In short, thingness has nothing to do with a cognitive realism that
affirms the reality of the external world and its transcendence
with respect to thinking. The type of knowledge to which the sex
appeal of the inorganic initiates us is paradoxically closer to the
technological imagination than to epistemology, in the sense that
it does not worry so much about the conditions of objectivity of
its own experiences as about the search for extreme experiences
that widen both the horizons of feeling and knowledge.

Heidegger's meditation on the thing is intrinsically sexual
because thing is another name for reliability (*Verlassigkeit*).

Trusting, entrusting, are constitutive of thingness, they are not added to it as something that can be or cannot be there, something that comes later, or is additional. I cannot rely on a mere instrument or entrust myself to it. What is a mere means ceases to be from the moment the purpose has been achieved, while the thing is an end in itself that remains as such at any moment and in any condition. If sexuality had orgasm and pleasure as its purpose, it could never become a horizon from which experience, philosophy and culture could acquire a sense. In the same way, if sexuality were only the object of specific knowledge, namely sexology, it would never constitute the essential aspect of an adventure from which our relationship with knowledge could emerge completely transformed. To say that the thing is reliability entails bending the entire semantic–conceptual field that revolves around the notion of faith, from ultramundane spirituality, to which it is traditionally connected, and from subjective humanism, in which modern thought has plunged it, towards an essentially terrestrial direction. In fact, for Heidegger the reliability of things refers to something certain that in the essay 'The Origin of the Work of Art' (*Der Ursprung des Kunstwerkes*) he calls earth or terrestrial: 'To determine the thing's thingness [...] we must aim at the thing's belonging to the earth.'[11] The novelty introduced by Heidegger in philosophy seems to be that we have to place our trust not in the divine or the human but in the mode of being of the thing. The link between philosophy and sexuality is founded precisely on this intuition because it is impossible to give oneself as a sentient thing without trusting in those who receive us, as it is impossible to take a sentient thing without feeling that it has trust in us. We have to look to medieval philosophy to find some precedent for the encounter between faith and thingness. In *The Thing* (*Das Ding*), Heidegger refers to Meister Eckhart, the theologian in whose work, for instance, we can find the use of the word 'thing' with reference to God and the soul. But it is clear in this case that the thing is part of a mystic vision of the world that seems to neglect the earth entirely. Perhaps it is also useful to remember that Arab philosophers, and in particular Avicenna, posed the problem of quiddity, *mahiyya*, at the centre of a questioning on the essence of being. It would be interesting to know whether in Semitic languages the relation between thing and being is posited in a more earthly and concrete way than in Western mysticism, which is saturated with Neoplatonism. Within the framework of the great cultural traditions that have emerged in Western thought, the link between thing and faith seems marginal, if not extraneous, to the Greeks, if not to Judaism. If anything, it is in the Roman world, in the union of Roman juridical mentality and Stoicism, as the first philosophical style of Semitic origin, that one can trace the intuition of a relation between *res*, understood in the dynamic sense of question, practice, thing to be dealt with, and *bona fides*, trust, loyalty. After all, the idea that evil, deceit and the diabolical originate not so much from a fall in the material and historical world, but, on the contrary, from a lack of reality, thingness, from a too mobile, evanescent and captious spirituality, was widespread in the first centuries of Christianity among those like Tertullian whose Roman thinking was married to Stoicism. In other words, in the sex appeal of the inorganic, there is at work, underground, a type of sensibility which is especially excited by statues, simulacra, living pictures whose origins can be traced back to the Roman world, whose statuophilia and pygmalionism are not without their relation to Roman archaic religion characterized by ceremonies, rituals without myths, and practices that have power of law.

However, Heidegger never identifies man with thing. In the essay on the work of art, the earth, understood as 'self-closure' (*das Sichverschliessende*), par excellence, as something which is safe and trustworthy, is opposed to the world understood as the 'constantly unobjective' (*das immer Ungegenständliche*), as somewhat open and dangerous. Whereas things are closer to the earth, deprived of world and belonging to the surroundings of which they are part, man, on the other hand, has a world, a horizon which is inseparable from the opening of relations, the taking of decisions, the assumption of risks. In short, it seems that being has a closer relation to the thing and the earth than to man and the world. The latter are more conditioned from Nothing than from Being. After all, according to Heidegger, there is a constant struggle between earth and world which, despite bringing each one of them above what each one is, always asserts their specific essence. The experience to which the sex appeal of the inorganic introduces us, instead, is oriented by a convergence, if not by an indistinction between man and thing, whose final philosophical meaning appears undecided. What happens, in fact, starting from the moment when the neutral and impersonal sexuality of the thing that feels asserts itself as the key paradigmatic event around which society and contemporary culture revolves? An anthropologization of being, and, therefore, the fulfilment of the modern project that places man at the centre of the world and makes him lord and master of the earth, or, on the contrary, an ontologization of man, and, thus the introduction, at first sight, of his most subjective and empirical aspect, namely that of sexual feeling, in the neutral and impersonal territory of being? In other words, if the world becomes earth and earth world, what happens? A world similar to the one described by Bret Easton Ellis in the novel *American Psycho*, where danger, insecurity and the most gratuitous sexual crimes are everyday occurrences, or an earth similar to the planet Whileaway described in Joanna Russel's novel *Female Man*, peopled by women alone who are always working, where safety, reliability and prodigality reign? What is in store for us, a worldly earth or a world always available? Or neither?

In his later writings, Heidegger no longer opposes earth to world, and thinks of the earth and sky, divinities and mortals as included in an original unity that he defines with the term 'fouring' (*Geviert*).[12] In this reformulation of his thinking, the thing is emancipated from a relation of belonging together with the earth and acquires a wider and more general meaning. It unites in a relation and makes permanent the four terms of the fouring. In the etymological meaning of *Ding* and Thing there is implicit a reference to joining, to 'the enfolding clasp of their mutual appropriation' (p. 179), whose sexual implications certainly cannot escape us. Even more surprising is the new role that Heidegger assigns to the concept of world which, disengaged from any relation of competition with the earth, points rather to the play, the dynamic relation that occurs within the fouring. To say that 'the thing things' (*Das ding Dingt*) (p. 181) is not much different from saying that 'the world presences by world-ing' (p. 179). By these expressions, tautologically odd, Heidegger means to refer to a gathering and to a retaining common both to thing and world.

The thing and the world interpenetrate but, according to Heidegger, their relation can never be a fusion. In his view, it is impossible to state that man is a thing. The thing seems to be always a little higher or a little below man and the world, or at least a little detached from them. If man were to succeed to become a thing his pain would be over. Perhaps, only through sexuality can one succeed in overcoming this pain. Perhaps only in sexuality man becomes thing. But Heidegger's thinking avoids this conclusion. Between thing and world there remains a gap, an in-between (*Zwischen*). The thing reunites without abolishing the gap, narrows without abolishing the distance. The accent is placed on the inorganic character of the unity, on the insuppressibility of an in-between between Being and man, between things and language, on the enigma of a presence that contains in itself the nature of absence. That is why Heidegger's thinking places an insurmountable obstacle to the sex appeal of the inorganic. The abandonment (*Gelassenheit*) of things to things, which Heidegger proposes in the last instance, is also steeped in resignation with respect to the possibility of accessing their most essential way, to which poetic language alludes without being able to show it fully, that it lets appear without being able to make it shine.

23

Division and Sex Appeal
of the Inorganic

How can we write pages and pages on sexuality and related
matters without taking minimally into consideration femininity
and masculinity? Is not the neutral, by any chance, a masked male
who, in donning a mask, places himself above the parts and
pretends to avoid the war between the sexes? Or, on the contrary,
an apology for the sentient thing and without orgasm does it
not imply a castration of the male implied, a radical negation of
the specific character of his sexuality? And then, even agreeing
on the possibility of a feeling without desire, suspended and
philosophical, apathetic and ataractic, what does it have that is
specifically sexual? And finally, even admitting that there is a sex
appeal of the inorganic, is it not inevitable that within it the
distinction between male and female is reproduced, or, at least,
metaphorically identifiable in movements of give and take?

All these legitimate questions are based on the premise, given
as self-evident, that there are two sexes. Reflecting on this duality
two basic theories of sexuality have been developed. The first is
under the sign of unity: feminine and masculine are two com-
plementary opposites that try and tend to join together, thus
creating a unity which is ontologically superior to their division.
Sexuality, therefore, is considered as separation and desire for
union. However, of these two aspects, the second is much more
important than the first. In fact, the first aspect, from which
originates etymologically the word *sexus* (from *secare*: to cut,
divide), is not thought of at all unless as an unhappy condition
which one has to remedy by, precisely, re-establishing unity.
A much more refined variant than this first theory thinks of the
masculine and the feminine as two principles, two archetypes that

can be present within the same person. The mythological figure of the androgyne represents the harmonious co-presence of masculine and feminine in divine unity or in a past or future entity more perfect than the historical one. Now, androgyny seems to me as remote as one can imagine it to be from the sex appeal of the inorganic. It is the victory of organic unity over sexuality, metaphysics over neuter, thinking over feeling. Closer to the sex appeal of the inorganic is hermaphroditism, which implies the best possible way in which the characteristics of both sexes are contained in a figure, namely, a man with breasts or a woman with a penis. In fact, hermaphroditism does not place the accent so much on the unification of opposites as on their neutralization, indetermination and indefiniteness. The masculine and feminine are not exalted and celebrated together in a union that promotes both but, on the contrary, they tend to erase each other, to cancel each other reciprocally in something ambiguous and enigmatic that potentially can develop in one direction, or in its opposite. But precisely for this reason, the hermaphrodite body is an organic unity, which is extraneous to artificial feeling. Philosophical theories that deal with sexuality without speaking of sexual difference, such as that of Merleau-Ponty, seem to allude to a hermaphrodite body. It would be interesting to reflect on the possible relation between the phenomenological approach, inevitably connected to the primacy of conscience, and the idea of a non-neuter, non-thing-like sexuality, but neutral, that is, neither masculine nor feminine.

The second fundamental theory of sexuality does not aim at uniting the sexes but at recognizing their duality as something essential and ineliminable. However, it is very difficult to establish in what masculinity and femininity consist. From a biological point of view, we know that the genetic patrimony is characterized by an entire series of contradictory factors that dissolve the possibility of a univocal determination of being male and female. Sexology identifies thirteen criteria: chromosomal sex, chromatimic, drumstick sex, germ cells' sex, hormonal, hypothalamic, morphological, etc. From the psychological point of view, the dual association of the male with the active and the female with the passive seems to be a prejudice derived from

Aristotelian philosophy and its primacy of form over matter. Furthermore, it has no sense in speaking of passive drives because the drive is always active; what can be passive is only the destination. From the point of view of procreation, we can't see what it has to do with sexuality. Indeed, there is no need to wait for the sex appeal of the inorganic or for artificial insemination to separate sexuality from reproduction. The only perspective from which the dichotomy between male and female appears more plausible is that of social registration, that is, the separation of humanity between male and female that leads to their alliance or their war. But this is a political problem which is structured, in fact, on the relation between two symmetrical entities. One subscribes to a sex as one subscribes to a political party. Sexuality is thus inserted into a logic which is foreign to it. Of course, this does not exclude the fact that the war between men and women entails consequences that shape experience. By uniting the weapons of strength and those of weakness, for instance, women often introduce tactical elements that are foreign to traditional political conflict. On the opposite front, the attraction that transvestites exercise on men is often based on the reassurance of being able to find an ally under provocative feminine guises. But all this has very little to do with sexuality. Equally unsatisfactory is the theory of an essential bisexuality of all human beings and the infinite combinations that a different dosage of masculinity and femininity can create. Even though interesting for the great number of possibilities that it introduces, it still clings to the dichotomy between two principles whose essence continues to evade us.

An important version of the dualistic theory of sexuality is provided by psychoanalysis. In the works of Freud, Lacan, Luce Irigaray the division between masculine and feminine is thought of as asymmetric. According to Freud, the male–female opposition can be read in terms of the relation between phallic and castrated. Hence an identification of sexuality with the masculine which is taken to its extreme consequences by Lacan for whom there is no other sexual enjoyment beside the phallic. This theory is overturned by Irigaray whose work aims at asserting the difference of a femininity which is neither one nor two, and which constitutes therefore a kind of unthought which is not accessible either to the instruments of formal logic or to the logic of dialectics.

From this somewhat rapid review of the theories of sexuality, we can conclude that the sex appeal of the inorganic can be situated neither in a harmonizing perspective that considers unity as essential, nor in a dualistic perspective that attributes a decisive meaning to the duality of male and female. In general terms, both harmony and dichotomy do not succeed in avoiding the naturalist organicism that thinks of the libido on the model of hunger. Now, unlike a soul or a body, the thing that feels never has enough. Its sexual feeling is infinite and, thanks to this infinity, it extends to any form of art and culture in a kind of neutral and impersonal pan-sensualism. If the essence of sexuality consists in division, the sex appeal of the inorganic does not stop at the dichotomy between masculine and feminine but continues the division to infinity according to a procedure which is similar to that of infinitesimal mathematics. Inorganic sexuality is not able to understand why there should only be two sexes, and not as many sexes as there are numbers, that is, infinite sexes. But sexuality is as boundless as the infinite, understood as infinite divisibility of a given size, and shows its own implicit sexuality, in exceeding any limit and in appearing entirely available in its actuality. To be sure, one could object that one thing is the division between masculine and feminine, which poses an empirical qualification however confused and tangled, and another is a division that extends to infinity among ever smaller sizes entirely abstract and qualitatively indeterminable. But it is precisely abstraction and indetermination that transform an object into a thing, the organ into something inorganic, natural and satisfiable sexuality into an artificial and infinite sexuality. As long as I perceive the exercise of sexuality as a filling of a cavity and being filled by a protuberance, everything is resolved in a division between empty and full, concave and convex, which, in any case, is nothing but the beginning of a process of division which is exercised on every part of my body and on the body of my partner. They are infinite because they are divisible to infinity. If I consider them as unitary and organic entities, what matters is their finiteness, the limit that delineates their shape. Thus I remain prisoner of a formal consideration that removes the possibility of grasping in me and in her the thing as thing. Only from the moment when I think of them as things divisible to infinity, their form falls apart and they are revealed as jewellery boxes, treasure chests of a treasure of infinite excitement.

After all, ever since antiquity, there have been two conflicting theories on the idea of division to infinity. The first goes back to Aristotle who denies the evidence of an actual infinite and claims the exclusive intelligibility of the limit. It aims at the formal and finite affirmation of any experience. The other, proposed by the Stoics, claims that all bodies can be divided to infinity and that man, as a result, is not made up of a greater number of parts than a finger, or the universe of a greater number of parts than man. As a result, there are no ultimate parts and the whole real is solid, continuous, not divided by a plurality of forms closed in themselves and separated from one another. The ultimate sense of infinite divisibility is clear here. It is not concomitant with a division and fragmentation of the real, but, on the contrary, with its consistency and contiguity. In the world there are no jumps, fractures or voids. The two sexes are within each one of us, but what is important is not their amount, as in the theory of human bisexuality, but the fact that each one of these two sexes is still divisible into two others and so on to infinity, so that within us there is an infinite number of sexes, and one moves from one to the other through a transit, a passing from the same to the same, without rupture. One could remark that only the parts of the first division have a name, namely masculine and feminine, while the others have no names. But we forget that neutral and inorganic sexuality does not rely on names and forms, but on things and numbers. What is paramount and essential is not the dichotomy between masculine and feminine, but the division in two parts divisible to infinity. The excitement of the sex appeal of the inorganic is nourished by abstraction and analysis. It captures the essence of sexuality a lot better than organic libido, devised on the model of hunger. Sex is not the incorporation or the being incorporated by the symmetrical opposite, rather *secare*, that is, dividing without ever halting in this division.

A very important trend in contemporary mathematics is closer to the Stoic thesis of infinite division than to the Aristotelian negation of the infinite. The greatest theoretician of the existence of actual infinity is Georg Cantor, the author of a theory of transfinite numbers which is inseparable from the statement of the primacy of continuity. It is curious that mathematical reflection can shift the questioning on sexuality from the relation between 1 and 2, between androgynous unity and the war of the sexes, to what lies in between 0 and 1. In the infinite space of this in-between there are infinite sexes, whose accessibility depends exclusively on the neutral, impersonal, inorganic experience of sexuality. Mathematics and inorganic sexuality are revealed to be strictly intertwined almost as if the enquiry on the nature of numbers provoked an excitement similar to that of a thing that feels. The latter does not possess at all the dimension and form of an object, or of a body. It should rather be thought of as something infinitesimal. The non-standard analysis, proposed by Abraham Robinson, provides very fine conceptual instruments to think the extremely little. The theorem of compactness that accompanies it constitutes under certain aspects a reformulation of the principle of continuity.

If from these abstract formulations we attempt to shift to more empirically intuitive representations, we are reminded of the Dionysian *sparagmos*, the dismembering of the body of the sacrificial victim. But leaving aside the macabre and horrifying character of this practice, it is legitimate to ask whether or not it is directed by an organicist drive that aims at establishing and renewing the unity of a unique vital energy. He who has spent an entire night tearing in ever smaller and minute pieces the dress worn by his lover the first time he possessed her, to the point of ripping the skin of the hands, and falling exhausted on a heap of shreds, threads, buttons and dust, has perhaps come closest to the inorganic feeling of sexual division. But if all this dismembering of clothes was done in an uncontainable burst of rage, anger and outrage, he has incommensurably distanced himself from neutral and impersonal sexuality, to which precisely that dress had introduced him. By being constituted as an indignant and outraged subject, he has failed the *epochē*, the indifference, the suspension of desire that constitutes the sine qua non condition of the sex appeal of the inorganic. That night did not see the actual good infinity of sexual division, but the bad potential infinity of having to be that is not, of life that runs after the unreachable, of spirit that longs for an impossible liberation. Only by putting together one by one the very tiny shreds of the dress on the naked body of one's lover can one reach once again that abandonment of things that makes possible the access to the sex appeal of the inorganic. In the transit that goes from the cloth to the skin, and from the skin to the cloth, one can re-establish the experience of a neutral and inorganic sexuality. It is sympathetic with a suspension of objects of desire, with an abstract excitement that never tires of operating infinite divisions on one's own body and that of one's partner.

And as to the give and take, the sex appeal of the inorganic abolishes their opposition which is meaningful only within the sphere of an organic sexuality thought of on the model of hunger. A thing that feels gives and takes at the same time through a single act. In ancient Greek, the verb *dechomai* contains, precisely, this ambiguity of meanings. It means to accept, to receive, to welcome, but also to take in the sense of to attract and to keep. This ambiguity exists also in similar words in other languages, but *dechomai* is connected with a dimension of reciprocity inherent in the relation that intervenes between guests and with an experience of mutual and vast availability.

24

Inclusive Metawritings

How can literature, which narrates life, describes the world, manifests subjectivity, turn into something inorganic, lose the transparency of expression and representation, become an accomplice of a neutral and impersonal experience? How can the word become thing? And yet in literature the rejection of organicity and living occurred a lot earlier than in music, architecture and the figurative arts. The indetermination under the guise of the disappearance of the author and anonymity, the porosity that emerges as open work, the exteriority understood as rebellion to metaphysical spiritualism implicit in a phonetic conception of language are similar aspects of a process of neutralization and reification of the word which has been studied in an exemplary way by Michel Foucault, Umberto Eco and Jacques Derrida. This process whose beginnings go back to the second half of the nineteenth century is characterized by the opposition between an instrumental language, hetero-referential, subordinate to what it wants to communicate, and an opaque, autonomous language, whose essential aspect is self-referentiality. What in the last instance exemplifies the literariness of a book and constitutes the text as such is the combination of devices through which writing refers to itself, to the modalities of its production and its fruition, the difference of its stature with respect to utilitarian writings and subject to having to transmit messages. It would seem, then, that poetry is such only on condition of being the poetry of poetry, narrative on condition of being the novel of novel, according to devices of doubling, self-reflection, self-representation similar to those studied and practised by philosophical research. The paths of literature and philosophy cross and interconnect in the experience of a metawriting that originates and develops on the ceaseless questioning of its own possibility.

However, this reification of the literary word poses two problems. The first can be formulated as follows: Why does this movement of self-reflection, of the word's turning on itself seem to us a becoming thing and not, instead, a spiritualization of literature, or its immersion in a vitalistic current that captures life in its immediate presence, in its vibrating here and now? If the characteristics of metaliterature are self-reflection, the acquisition of a 'for itself', of a self-consciousness, are not these, precisely, the peculiar traits of the organic as Hegel defines it? Or must we surmise that German speculative philosophy is incapable of understanding thingness as such, precisely because it places life and spirit above everything? As a result, is any attempt to understand metaliterature according to speculative thought bound to failure? Should we not rather question the linguistic–semiotic notion of language in order to understand the being thing of language? But, in so doing, are we not transferring a philosophical–literary problem to a context that ignores the distinction between thing and object, that posits the meta-linguistic function beside the others without granting it any privilege, which reduces the experience of the thing that feels to a question of psycholinguistic competence?

The second problem, which is even more complex, concerns the relationship between language and sexuality. The sex appeal of the inorganic ushers a neutral and impersonal feeling, an artificial sexuality independent of the natural dynamic of desire and its satisfaction. It intuits that this pretext presents an affinity with the metaliterary adventure of the twentieth century, of which it admires the character of an extreme experience, its radicality and refusal to compromise. However, it is aware that the poetry of poetry and the novel of novel have proceeded according to a mechanism of exclusion that has progressively thrown out and expelled all hetero-referential linguistic materials, which turned out to be extraneous to the purity of its intent. Hence a desexualization, an ascesis of literature of which Samuel Beckett is the extreme example. Without doubt he reached a neutral and impersonal writing, but this result which is founded on an *epochē*, on a suspension of the entire real, puts the writer in a rarefied and desexualized climate. In short, it seems as if metawriting and inorganic sexuality are in a relation of competition, as two competitors who are playing the same game, pursuing the same strategy of suspending life and which for this reason will never meet. The connection between language and sexuality has been, instead, emphasized by psychoanalysis which by positing itself as inheritor of a will to knowledge, of a *scientia sexualis*, which has its roots in the practice of religious confession, has instituted an interpretative system within which the libido reigns supreme. The sex appeal of the inorganic finds itself likewise in a competitive relation with psychoanalysis, by virtue of the common project of sexualization of the linguistic universe.

Literature thus reveals itself to be the crucial place of *philosophia sexualis*, the place in which the latter is besieged on the one hand by linguistics, which wants to de-legitimize it at the level of language, on the other by psychoanalysis that wants to delegitimize it at the level of sexuality. Furthermore, philosophy entertains, naturally, a more essential relation with literature than with music, architecture or the figurative arts, because it is made of words – better, of few words that return, such as poetry's, in obsessive ways in different contexts. It is obligated to a rigorous self-discipline and to processes of exclusion no less rigid than those at work in metaliterature. For example, I am at chapter number twenty-four of a book whose topic is sexuality without having been able to deal yet with the question that seems the most obvious, the relation between sex and pleasure. The difference between philosophical rhetoric, which considers philosophy books as mere transcription of oral discourses – for instance, of university lectures or participation in round-table discussions – and philosophical writing, which considers the textual aspect, the system of connections, variations, references, plots that unify and structure a philosophical composition as a decisive aspect for its comprehension, always turns out to be more profound. I would also add that a *philosophia sexualis* is possible only at the moment when the word is viewed as a thing that feels, which has its autonomy not only with respect to what it means, but above all with respect to the framework of opinions, intentions, vague beliefs and equally vague reminiscences that keep together the philosophizing subject. Writing encounters inorganic sexuality on condition of exceeding the philosopher's knowledge. It seems that one can access the enigma of what one does not know, what one feels, who one feels and why, only when one does not know what one writes, who writes and why. The encounter of philosophy with sexuality, which probably represents the new great game of Western thought, not only goes through literary writing but is not even thinkable without it, without the great adventure that has transformed poems and novels into self-referential things.

To be sure this adventure has been in large part guided by the search for an absolutely pure language, that has nothing to do with the instrumentality of everyday usage. Therefore it has created a gap between a literature which is exclusive and self-aware and a literature of consumption whose tendency is to represent and narrate the world, more or less naively. Therefore, paradoxically, its claim to being thing turns out to be thwarted precisely by the process of exclusion that characterized it. The result, therefore, has been a more solemn, a more organic and aural work than ever, a quintessence of spirit and life very distant from the indeterminate, porous and external mode of being of things. This event, which begins, curiously, with two authors, Poe and Baudelaire, who under some aspects can be considered among the principal promoters of the collective imaginary of the masses, came to an end during the early sixties. Its place was taken by another type of metaliterature that does not proceed by exclusion but by inclusion, which gathers the most disparate linguistic elements, and reproduces without assimilating them, organically – documents, inscriptions, acts, prescriptions, certificates, registers, graffiti, bulletins, notices, announcements, bans, posters, signs, marks, warnings derived from everyday life. All these elements are not organic parts of a wider whole. In fact, even in this case, as it was with sexual division, mathematics is the style of thought that can provide us with adequate conceptual models to clarify the logical course of the inorganic. The theory of sets, mereology, the protothetics of Stanislaw

Lésniewski, introduce us to problematics that think of inclusion in an entirely independent way from spiritualist and naturalist premises. For instance, the distinction between one-dimensional distributive classes, founded on finite cardinal numbers, and multidimensional collective classes, containing elements or subsets of different nature among them, turns out to be quite relevant to understanding the mechanism of inclusive metaliterature. The ultimate sense of these mathematical inventions can always be traced back to the main experience of inorganic sexuality, namely, dissolving forms, valorizing principles of continuity and transitivity, transiting from element to element without hiatuses or breaks, undermining the primacy of genital and organic sexuality, sexualizing the world.

Georges Perec is the writer whose long reflection on things has led to a novel of more than five hundred pages, *La vie mode d'emploi*, which appears to be one of the most radical examples of inclusive metaliterature. The structure of the book is provided by spatial, architectural data. Perec imagines a Parisian apartment whose façade is removed from the basement to the attic making all the rooms simultaneously visible. Next he goes on to narrate the lives and to describe the activities of the dwellers. The novel's metanarrative character consists in the fact that it is constructed as a puzzle made up of ninety-nine chapters within which multiple stories, classifications, directories, quotations, references interweave, branch off, overlap and develop according to mechanisms of production sometimes self-evident, sometimes declared, sometimes respected, sometimes transgressed. The general effect of this immense and enigmatic work is that of reification pushed to extreme consequences. The 'life' alluded to in the title includes an infinity of things, different from one another, whose general sense seems justified by a common mania of collecting, classifying and preserving.

What is absent in Perec's wonderful work is precisely the dimension of sexuality, almost as if it belonged by essence and definition to that spiritual and vital dimension that he means to deny in the most categorical way. His writing is not so much ascetic as asexual. His things do not achieve feeling. Why? Is it, perhaps, because only when words are invested with philosophical thinking that they succeed in acquiring that mobility, that pregnancy, that emotional rapidity which makes them capable of unleashing a neutral and abstract excitement? Is there a linguistic hyperaesthesia connected with the practice of an abstract language, such as the philosophical or mathematical one? Why do I find the expression 'inclusive metawriting' more loaded with sexual intensity than most obscene words? Perhaps the attraction exercised by metaliterary devices depends precisely on the impression that by their means writing acquires a kind of autonomous sensibility with respect to the writer and the reader. Now inorganic sexuality resembles this kind of sentient book which receives and makes room for all languages, enters into them and bends them by making them reflect themselves. Inclusive metawriting is revealed, thus, as a metasexuality without either subject or form, in which the single body is changed in the extension of another's body. It acknowledges and transforms everything by removing materials from whatever context and suspending them in a field crossed by continuous tensions.

To be sure, the becoming sex of philosophy is not separable from its becoming writing. It is starting from the problems of the philosophical text that a very wide horizon of literary experimentation opens up, in which mingle technical questions of philosophical terminology, inquiries on the plurality and the specificity of languages, extreme experiences of depersonalization and neutralization, and the most inclusive and absorbing attempts of collective production. When we say today that the philosopher is above all a writer, one should add that writing has become, in the meantime, something different from how it was practised and developed by the 'great writers' of the nineteenth and twentieth centuries.

25

Wittgenstein and the Feeling of 'this thing'

Seminal in Wittgenstein's observations on psychology is the reference to a particular type of experience that shows hidden and substantial affinities with the neutral sexuality of the sex appeal of the inorganic. Wittgenstein did not define this experience unequivocally which, besides, holds no apparent relation to sexuality or philosophy. It consists in seeing an entity that remains unchanged now as one thing and now as another. The simplest and clearest example is provided by a design which, according to the way we look at it, is now the head of a hare and now the head of a duck. In actuality, there are many things that provide us with this impression of ambiguity. First of all works of art, such as musical pieces that we now listen to in one way, now in another, or buildings, sculptures and paintings from which we now receive one emotion now another. But even more prosaically, the objects of everyday life can also generate different reactions. Not even geometrical figures are exempt from this ambiguity, as in the case of the triangle that now can be seen resting on its base, now hanging from its vertex. Finally, language turns out to be the place for excellence of this experience because there is no such thing as univocal correspondence between words and things. The same terms allow for infinite linguistic plays that surprise us constantly, creating a feeling of estrangement and unnaturalness. Even the most familiar places can seem suddenly uncanny. The room where I have lived for years suddenly appears to me under a different guise. And what about people? A man can be a perfect enigma to another, but, even worse, there is the continuing difficulty in recognizing people to whom one has been close for a long time.

There is a very simple and common explanation to all these psychological phenomena. We say that a thing, that could very well be either a triangle or your wife, while remaining the same, can be interpreted differently. But Wittgenstein rejects this solution categorically because the examples mentioned earlier do not concern conceptual processes, mental actions, but visions and sensations. The strangeness lies in the fact that I see, feel, perceive the same thing in a different way from the way I used to see it, feel it and perceive it before; without that this change can be rationally comprehensible. In fact, it remains *this thing* which is before me. If I attributed a determining importance to the mental aspect of perception, to its formal organization, I would no longer be able to see 'something *as something*'[13], but something as an absurdity, a non-thing (*Unding*) or, even, as absolutely nothing (*not a thing*).

Wittgenstein is particularly interested in the rapidity of the process through which I see something under a new aspect, the sudden lightening of a new feeling, the assertion, in a sensorily indisputable way, of an unforeseen and unexpected sensation. How is it that I can see in the same design, at the same time, a hare instead of a duck? How is it that this new aspect is accompanied by a greater intensity, a sparkling, the lighting of its semblance? We should not judge Wittgenstein's infinite questioning negatively, as the questioning of every certainty. This is only the critical part of his thought which acquires vigour and importance with relation to a positive part which, even though not explicit and apparent, bursts here and there with great energy. Thus, seeing something, now as one thing now as another, is a marginal experience only with respect to a common feeling, which is blind to the sparkling, just as some are blind to seeing or lack a musical ear. If thinking were speech as Plato claims, it would lack completely that lightning rapidity that allows us to utter the phrases: 'Now I can!' or 'All is changed!'

But what is the relation between the surprise of seeing something under a new aspect and the sex appeal of the inorganic? Wittgenstein's search, oriented toward a new way of feeling, finds itself before two psychological theories that prevent the access to a new sensorial and emotional world. The first is the spiritualist, subjectivist and mentalist one that goes back to Descartes and extends to the psychology of form and beyond, according to which feeling is ascribable to mental representations and formations. The second theory is behavioural and positivistic, which by eliminating any reference to consciousness and by denying any validity to the introspective method reduces the importance of feeling to what can be objectively observed. Wittgenstein rejects both the theory of the primacy of the spirit and that of the body, and attempts to open up a new horizon of feeling where the barriers between organic and inorganic are overcome. The pain for him becomes THIS THING, written just like that in capital letters (I, no. 263, p. 93), that is, something which is resolved neither in a mental image nor in action, and which goes beyond both the word 'pain' and the scream. The thing 'pain' is perhaps more similar to a thing, a doll, a stone or a stove, to quote his examples, than to the mind or the machine of the body. The thing 'pain' does not think and does not work. 'I turn to stone and my pain goes on. – Suppose I were in error and it was no longer *pain*?' (I, no. 288, p. 98). This questioning contains the problematic of inorganic sexuality. In fact, if I petrify myself I access a type of sensibility which is beyond pain, for which the painful experience is inadequate. 'What gives us *so much as the idea* that living beings, things, can feel?' (I, no. 283, p. 97). Perhaps the fact that we are no longer aware of the difference between men and things? Perhaps our feeling finds as little correspondence and comprehension in other human beings as it finds in a doll, a stone or a stove? Perhaps the idea that others understand what we feel derives from an animistic belief that attributes sensations and feelings to them. However, if we follow this chain of hypotheses, the point of arrival is a psychic solipsism from which there is no escape. Often Wittgenstein gives the impression of being walled in in his pain. Derek Jarman, in his film *Wittgenstein*, has portrayed this aspect very well, as well as the relation between philosophy and masochism, thought and suffering.

Instead of closing myself in the blind alley of masochistic solipsism, I could imagine myself transformed into a stone. 'In what sense will *the stone* have the pains?', Wittgenstein asks,

'And why need the pain have a bearer?' (I, no. 283, p. 97). With this question Wittgenstein goes beyond the mind–body dichotomy and opens up the space of neutral and impersonal feeling. It is no longer relevant to know who feels pain, whether I or the stove. This thing pain would acquire an autonomous character and become independent of its attribution to a subject. Sensation would have pre-eminence with respect to him who attributes it to himself. According to Wittgenstein, many different criteria of personal identity exist: 'Now which of them determines my saying that "I" am in pain? None' (I, no. 404, p. 122). In this answer, however, there is something unsatisfactory that stems from the particular type of feeling to which Wittgenstein constantly refers. In fact, it is difficult to claim that pain could be something impersonal. If one wants to desubjectivize feeling, one must suspend the four fundamental passions: pleasure, pain, desire and fear.

Here neutral and impersonal sexuality plays a decisive role. In fact, it is strictly connected with that sense of extraneity and unnaturalness that Wittegenstein attributes to the perception of something *as something* and not nothing, of *this thing* as an entity that surprises, flashes and glows. As long as I remain within organic sexuality, I feel familiar and natural things such as ecstasies and orgasms, pleasures and pains, desires and fears. But all these forms of feeling are mental representations or standardized behaviours, whose sincerity is always in doubt. They are non-things through which one is under the illusion of understanding and communicating. Only when my body and that of my partner lose their obviousness as animated and functioning bodies, as expressive and representative forms, as instruments characterized by the attainment of precise goals, do they become this coloured and lively thing, capable of arousing infinite excitement. The entrance to the sex appeal of the inorganic makes one slightly dizzy, as when one executes an acrobatic feat; it seems accompanied by a lightning flash, as when we finally come up with the right word after having searched for it for a while; it plunges feeling in an endless bewilderment; and – why not say it? – it gives us the experience of reality. To be sure, all this also applies to sounds, spaces, objects, words. When they are removed from being useful, they acquire an indeterminate, cooler and brighter aspect. Unfortunately, aesthetics, namely, the fact of considering them works of art, blurs and clouds their extraneous and unusual character. Therefore, not art but only sexuality can make us see and feel the thing as thing. The sex appeal of the inorganic is the teacher of excitement and of igniting sensations, not the aesthetic! Sounds, spaces, objects and words become *this thing* only incidentally. I begin to feel a music, a building, a sculpture, a poem as a thing, only if I have felt a cock, a cunt, a hand, an eye as thing.

Neutral sexuality, not pain, supplies us with reality as special effect. As long as I remain in pain, it is impossible to escape the alternative between the doubt as to what others really feel and private certitude, which cannot be communicated and is solipsistic of him who says to himself: 'I know what I mean!' In inorganic sexuality these problems do not exist because the forms of subjective feeling are replaced by an impersonal 'one feels'. But how does one feel? One feels together with extreme evidence and suspension, as in a kind of coloured and intense *epochē*. Wittgenstein describes the phenomenon whereby a word heard out of context, for instance only for a brief moment, now has a meaning and soon after another, and defines this condition as a *Vorschweben*, 'a matter of something standing or stirring in front of one's eyes'.[14] Now the verb *schweben* means to soar, to be suspended. Therefore, contrary to what at first may appear, suspension is not attenuation, reduction of the force of perception, but, on the contrary, it is a condition of its igniting, its sparkling, its shining. *This thing* radiates.

26

Pleasure and Sex Appeal of the Inorganic

And now we come to the saddest topic of this book: pleasure! It is already difficult to separate desire from sexuality, but to free it from pleasure seems almost impossible at first. There are always lovers of pleasure to wave the flag of sexuality so that one has difficulty in talking about sex without being implicated in their sugary and sickly vulgarity. In fact, hedonism is characterized by an inane and conceited idleness, an indolent and mellifluous self-complacency, a self-important and obtuse enervation which is only capable of bragging of its own *savoir-vivre*, its ability to pass from enjoyment to enjoyment, its talent for tasting all the delights that life has to offer! And yet there is nothing in pleasure that connects it univocally and certainly to sexuality. All the defenders of pleasure are more or less, openly or secretly, partially or entirely, enemies of sexuality, especially when it is not content with staying natural and organic, but conquers its autonomy and radicality in the neutral and infinite experience of the sex appeal of the inorganic.

The ancients, beginning with Aristippus of Cyrene and his followers, the Cyrenaics, have stated all there is to say about pleasure. They were called the 'refined' and they stood in antithesis to the Cynics whose model of conduct was inspired by the greatest austerity. Now Aristippus was not a dissolute man but a philosopher above all, a pupil of Socrates, and the only one to establish an inseparable link between knowledge and pleasure, and claim to appreciate physical enjoyment without reserve. In his view, the experience of the world gives us no certainty, and the autonomous activity of the mind is no less deceitful. There is only one certainty, only one firm point in life, namely, the fact that here and now we feel pleasure or pain. And we can state it with all the more certainty, the more we refer to our own body, the absolute positiveness of its testimony. The mind can be deviated by memory or expectation, but the body does not deceive us. We cannot say anything certain about the external causes of this pleasure or this pain, but on the intimate truth of these affections there is for Aristippus no doubt whatever. I feel pleasure or pain, therefore I am. Pleasure and pain are movements. The first one, soft, as the waves on a calm sea, the second, harsh, as the waves on a stormy sea. These are motions that occur within ourselves and in whose regard it is not possible to establish either a measure or a hierarchy. Since, by introducing calculus, arithmetic, or the plus and minus in affections, one undermines and compromises the absolute certainty of pleasure and pain, one renders them relative and introduces into the incontrovertible truth of corporeal testimony the doubts and uncertainties of mental processes. That is why, according to Aristippus, there is no difference among pleasures, they are all the same.

The two affections, pleasure and pain, for Aristippus, are not on equal terms. Although both are equally secure and, at the same time, preserve us from error, as they do not depend on sensation, which can be deceitful, but on a kind of internal infallible tact, nonetheless only pleasure is the goal of human existence. However, it cannot be the object of a choice because it would mean reaffirming the primacy of the mind over body. Pleasure has a surplus of reality, an excess of ontological positivity, so to speak, with respect to pain. According to the Cyrenaics, pleasure is more proper to us, more familiar, ever since childhood, without any choice or calculation on our part. In fact, pleasure is a way of feeling ourselves internally, of making us feel for ourselves with an obviousness and a gaiety that has no equal. Therefore, even though it is corporeal by definition, it cannot be determined and specified in an empirical way and remains, essentially, a philosophical experience, linked to knowledge and truth. We do not know whether Aristippus privileged one particular pleasure of the body over the others. It is never said whether pre-eminence should be given to eating, copulating, or any other activity. In fact, the essential is to understand that all the pleasures are equal. What is important is the intimate certainty of their truth, the only one we can arrive at. Aristippus holds onto the self-evidence of pleasure proper, and he clings to this one point after having left everything else to the mercy of doubt and uncertainty. From his point of view, the fact that we give pleasure to others is a lot less evident, so it is really unfair to consider his philosophy obscene.

The pleasure of which Aristippus speaks, already in antiquity, evoked the image of a siege, where, having put aside outside things, one locked oneself up in one's own affections, concentrating exclusively on them. Pleasure, thus, turns out to be the only experience of being, but it does not tell us how it is brought about and it cannot be communicated to others. According to the Cyrenaics, I know that I feel pleasure but I cannot affirm that there exists a pleasurable object or transmit my affection to others. I am entirely enclosed within myself. The image to which pleasure refers is that of a body without openings or where all openings have been sown up, as in *imbunche*, the evil spell worked by Araucanian witch doctors of which the Chilean writer José Donoso speaks in his novel *The Obscure Bird of Night*. This spell closes the nine openings of the human body and transforms it into a bag of skin and flesh which is blind and deaf-mute. Pleasure, in fact, seems to exclude penetration. The only movement to which it refers is entirely internal to the single body and concerns its quality alone, the fact of being light or harsh, calm or troubled, smooth or rough. It does not depend on sight, on hearing or any other sensation that implies a perception of the external world.

Hedonistic solipsism reaches its peak with Hegesias, a philosopher of the Cyrenaic school, known by the nickname of 'persuader of death'. In fact, the greatest intimacy with oneself can only be achieved with death. After all, isn't pleasure ceasing to be strong, abandoning oneself on a bed to the devouring voluptuousness of doing absolutely nothing, finally finding in unlimited starvation the reward for so much empty and senseless bustling about for oneself and others? The advantages we can obtain, according to Hegesias, are never worth what they cost. Life's balance is always in the red and the remuneration one receives is always disproportionately inferior to the energy one employs. In the quiet and silent secrecy of the tomb, our body can finally abandon itself to eternal enjoyment. Whoever lets himself die of starvation can entrust his own corpse to parents and friends binding them not to burn it or scatter it, but to bury it in a secluded place, leaving it to the calm and peaceful movement of decomposition. It is precisely in the collected intimacy of death that the internal touch, without any longer being distracted by sensations that come from outside, acquires the eternal possession of its truth. Feeling being dead is finally sinking in a feeling purified by the murkiness of human relations. This feeling is the ultimate model for all pleasures, whereas copulation, eating, drinking and discharging one's bowels are pale prefigurations by comparison. Of all the pleasures of life, the sexual is without doubt the most ambiguous because it distracts from the full enjoyment of oneself and leads toward sentiments that entail relations with others, toward doing things that please them, being a friend and ally, and being of help to them. And even though he will have received great advantages from others, these pleasures are never equal to those that he will have given himself. That is why sexual pleasure is the most deceitful of all. It makes us believe that we give and receive something, while pleasure is the most intransitive thing that exists. Only fools believe that they can help or damage others, that they can be useful or harmful, that they can give pleasure or suffering. The sage, according to Hegesias, does everything for himself. For him to live or die is indifferent because the greatest pleasure is dying, rather than being dead.

The Cyrenaics in 4 BC raised a great debate on the nature of pleasure and its relation to sexuality and knowledge, to which most of the philosophers of the time contributed. The different solutions given to the problem have marked the point of departure of positions that have been developed to this day. The possible answers to the hedonistic solipsism of the Cyrenaics are fundamentally two. The first upholds the relation between philosophy and pleasure established by Aristippus, but reforms the notion of pleasure by introducing socializing elements that exclude or strongly limit sexuality. This is the direction followed in different ways by Plato, Aristotle and Epicurus. The second answer, instead, claims that philosophy has nothing to do with pleasure and that this experience must be avoided at all costs. This is the course followed by another student of Socrates, Antisthenes, and later by Cynics and Stoics. The first road saves pleasure but not sexuality. Plato, Aristotle and Epicurus aim for a desexualized pleasure. The second road is, without doubt, ascetic and rigorous, but paradoxically it opens up unforeseen horizons where sexuality without pleasure can become a philosophical experience, precisely, that of the sex appeal of the inorganic. I will state briefly the ideas of the friends of pleasure; as for the enemies of pleasure, this entire book is a development of their ideas.

For Plato sexual pleasure is 'most false' but he does not deny pleasure altogether. Plato proposes an aesthetic reform of pleasure whose influence continues to this day. It consists, on the one hand, in breaking the relation between pleasure and sexuality, on the other, in linking pleasure with the beautiful. The introduction of the concept of the beautiful is what allows the escape from the solitude of hedonism. The beautiful introduces us to an experience that can be shared with others. Unlike the inner touch, the beautiful is something social, something on which we can form a judgement, that has characteristics similar to those that we formulate on truth and the good. The connection between pleasure and the beautiful seems obvious – in reality, it is Plato's invention. There is nothing in the notion of pleasure that by itself makes us prefer a beautiful girl to an ugly one. To make this distinction it is necessary to specify a certain type of pleasure, aesthetic pleasure. From the position of the beautiful as value originates a discrimination against those who are ugly, old, handicapped, which from the point of view of pleasure as such have no foundation.

The Platonic reform of the concept of pleasure is based on the search for true pleasure. It has the following characteristics: it implies the privileging of sight and hearing with respect to the other senses, it is stable, pure, measured and aware. In the first place, true pleasure can derive only from sight and hearing. According to Plato, it is ridiculous to think that sensations deriving from taste and touch can be defined as beautiful. As to sexual pleasures, precisely the fact that they are practised in private without witnesses constitutes proof that they have nothing to do with the beautiful. Thus a hierarchy is born between noble senses (sight and hearing), which make possible a true experience of pleasure, and senses that allow experiences that cannot be defined beautiful, because they are not socializing, but individual and private. This discrimination between aesthetic and non-aesthetic senses has lasted till today. The attempt by others to invent an aesthetic of the third sense, smell, clash in front of a fundamental problem. How can smell become a sense on which a common judgement is possible, on which one can establish a consensus? Even if this were possible, the fact remains that it is not objectifiable, that is it cannot be individualized in an object, but tends to incorporate it. Even more problematic is the establishment of a relation between taste and the beautiful. In this case the aspect of incorporation is even more evident and essential. As for touch, it seems the furthest from the notion and the experience of the beautiful. In ancient philosophy, the Stoics have attributed to touch a fundamental role, relating to it all the other four senses. But they opened a course which is opposite both to Aristippus and Plato, moving against both pleasure and the beautiful.

Secondly, for Plato, true pleasure is different from false pleasures, because it is stable. The conception of pleasure as movement makes it dependent on negative states such as need and desire. It transforms life into a continuous flow, in an incessant filling and voiding. According to Plato, pleasure implies a certain experience of stability and fullness. Pleasure in motion describes the life of a plover, a bird so greedy that it eats and discharges at the same time. After all, the beautiful was thought by the Greeks as something stable. They opposed the notion of beautiful (*to kalon*) to that of convenience (*to prepon*) which implies, instead, adapting to occasions and circumstances.

Thirdly, pleasure is different from false pleasures because it is pure. If pleasure is the satisfaction of a need or the gratification of a desire, it is not only pleasure but also the experience of a lack, namely pain. In fact, false pleasures are a mixture of pleasure and pain. In general, great pleasures are those characterized by wild excitement, by the simultaneous presence of opposite sensations, as when shuddering we flare up, or when burning we shiver from the cold. For Plato, if we want to observe great pleasures we must turn our attention more towards illness than towards health. In fact it is with the sick that pleasure reaches the greatest intensity. It makes the body tighten, makes it jump and produces in it all sorts of colours, shapes and puffing, and generates a general depression that causes insane screams. But in these experiences, in which one almost feels like dying, pleasure is never pure, but mixed with pain. Impure pleasures, therefore, cannot be true pleasures, because they are always mixed with pain. If we are looking for pure pleasure, for Plato, we must turn not to great but to small pleasures, which are connected to the experience of the beautiful. These are those that come from contemplating geometrical figures, the clear and even sounds that produce a harmonious melody, as well as the pleasure of learning, when it is not accompanied by the painful sensation of hunger for knowledge, and, finally, the pleasure that accompanies virtue.

But the most important aspect of pure pleasure is its measured, non-excessive, character. For Plato what qualifies the beautiful is precisely measure. One must keep away from all the pleasures that appear unlimited, infinite and insatiable. The pleasures that have neither measure nor end are surely false because they come from pain, are mixed with pain and bring pain. According to Plato, the pleasure of the beautiful is measured and can be measured. It keeps away from lack and from excess. The pleasure of the beautiful is linked to the exercise of reason. The sentence 'to be overcome by pleasure' has no sense for Plato. It would mean choosing a greater evil instead of a minor good. Whoever is overcome by pleasures, in fact, does not reason well, is not able to distinguish between pleasures, to differentiate pure and impure pleasure. Thus, Plato maintains the close relation between pleasure and philosophy established by Aristippus. A pleasurable life needs intelligence otherwise it would not even know how to enjoy it. Without true opinion you could not even think of enjoyment, and without the ability to calculate you could not even foresee what future you will enjoy. Plato's solution to exclude sexuality opens the way to academic aesthetics and establishes that particular type of pleasure without interest for the existence of the object that for Kant would be, precisely, aesthetic pleasure.

The way followed by Aristotle to escape the hedonistic prison is completely different from Plato's. He also reforms the notion of pleasure and affirms, even more strongly than Plato, the connection between philosophical knowledge and pleasure, but at the same time he rescues, at least partially, impure pleasure. For Aristotle, pleasure is not movement (*kinesis*), as Aristippus claimed, but action, activity (*energheia*). Movement tends to reach a purpose which is beyond action, which does not have an end in itself. Activity, instead, is perfect because, even though occurring in time, it has no development, or history, but is complete and adequate in itself. Pleasure, as activity, is accomplished in a single instant of time. By strictly linking the experience of pleasure to activity, the fundamental concept of his metaphysics, Aristotle gives it the greatest importance. It is the pivotal notion of his Ethics under which he considers both intellectual and physical activities. In his view, pleasure and life are inseparable. Without activity there is no pleasure and pleasure makes activity perfect.

His great philosophical strategy is based on the premise of a desensitization of pleasure. It is the activity of a disposition which conforms to nature, and is not hindered by the senses. This means that there can be a pleasure independent of the senses, in fact, the greatest pleasure is precisely the one connected to the exercise of reason. Are the pleasures of the body false pleasures? Not so, according to Aristotle, because the body also has an activity whose perfection is precisely pleasure. However, in the pleasures of the body we must distinguish between what represents a purely negative moment (such as putting an end to pain or satisfying a need) and what is, instead, the positive moment, the exercise of an activity. For Aristotle, eating, drinking and sexuality provide, doubtless, legitimate pleasures. The error, in his view, consists in considering these pleasures as the greatest, while in actual fact they are the smallest. Mistakenly, they seem the most desirable because of their negative character, because they drive pain away and satisfy needs. But this is not the essential aspect of pleasure.

If Plato's theory is an aesthetic reform of the notion of pleasure, Aristotle's theory is a metaphysical reform of pleasure. Discrimination with respect to ugly people, therefore, does not have an aesthetic but a metaphysical foundation. They are less perfect than the beautiful. At the basis of Aristotle's praise of pleasure, there is a metaphysical premise, namely, the ontological primacy of action over power, of activity over suffering, of form over matter, of soul over body, of man over woman, of thinking over feeling, of health over disease, of master over slave.

Aristotle's theory of pleasure was well received by Jacques Lacan because of the close connection with what analytic experience allows him to single out as the 'male side' of pleasure. According to Lacan, 'man does not come to enjoy the body of the woman precisely because what he enjoys is the enjoyment of the organ'.[15] Enjoyment, essentially male and phallic, cannot be shared with a woman. Once again pleasure is revealed as a prison.

The last great reform of pleasure in ancient philosophy is by Epicurus and could be defined as the theological way out of the hedonistic dead end. According to Epicurus, the gods are a kind of supermen. They are superworldly but not supernatural, they have analogous shapes to men, and are divided into masculine and feminine. Their number is not inferior to that of the human race. Their body is an almost body and their blood an almost blood. They live blessed and immortal without receiving or causing either pain or suffering, they are without anxiety or pain. If we wish to think about the nature of pleasure adequately, we have to take into account their way of being and feeling. They are not involved in any occupation, nor do they engage in any work, but they enjoy their wisdom and virtue. The task of philosophy is, precisely, that of introducing us into a way of being and feeling which is almost divine.

Epicurus rejects the dynamic conception of pleasure, both the Cyrenaic one as movement and the Aristotelian version as activity. For him, pleasure in movement is not pleasure, but only termination of pain and satisfaction of need. Pleasure, instead, is characterized by quietness, by the absence of anxiety. The greatest possible pleasure consists in the absence of fear and pain. Philosophy teaches us to conquer the greatest fear, that of death, by showing that man has nothing to fear. The study of nature has precisely this task. Even if man is not immortal, nonetheless, he can reach a state which is qualitatively similar to the divine.

What is striking in the Epicurean conception of pleasure is the emphasis on the passivity of simply letting oneself live. Sexuality is seen with suspicion. It is natural but not necessary, more of a cause for uneasiness than satisfaction. Worst of all is ambition, aspiring to power and glory, the search for excellent foods and drink. They increase the dependency on needs enormously. Finally, relations with others, which turn into friendship, are very important. It makes it possible to escape the isolation inherent in the Cyrenaic notion of pleasure. It asserts the idea of an alternative community with respect to institutions, founded on philosophical feeling.

Therefore, the relation with the other of which Epicurus speaks has more of a theological than a sexual emphasis. The similarity between Epicurus's notion of pleasure and the way in which Lacan speaks of feminine feeling, which he describes as a relation with the Other, that is, with God, is striking. It would seem, then, that male pleasure, thought of as activity, and feminine pleasure, thought of as openness to God, never meet. Enjoyment is characterized by an impasse that makes an actual 'relation' between the two sexes impossible. Everyone is enclosed in his or her own pleasure. The example given by Lacan to clarify his idea of feminine enjoyment is paradigmatic: 'It's Hadewijch of Antwerp, a church woman, one of those who are politely called a mystic'.

27

Perverse Performance

'I would rather go crazy than feel pleasure' Antisthenes used to say. Now the sex appeal of the inorganic is precisely the opposite of pleasure. Not pain, but an effort, an enterprise, an exercise, a training, a performance. Thus, not only sounds, spaces, objects and words free themselves from their relation with the spirit and life and become things that feel and that are felt, but also actions.

This transformation is inherent in the vicissitudes of the experimental theatre from the sixties onward. It begins with the emancipation from the primacy of the text and literature, with the challenge of the separation between actors and spectators, with the overcoming of the distinction between scene and reality. All this brings us to locate the essence of theatre in the exposition of an event that occurs here and now, in the flagrancy of its happening before our very eyes. At first sight this experience of the present, felt as something more intense and rousing than the fruition of traditional theatre, which is imitation of an action, not real action, seems to introduce us into a dimension characterized by greater spirituality and vitality. That is, it seems to move precisely in a direction opposite to neutral and suspended sexuality, toward an organic vitalism founded on collective participation. But this first impression is destined to be overturned in its opposite. In fact, unlike the representations of traditional theatre, the performance aims to be a unique event, irretrievable, irrevocable, unrepeatable and, precisely for these reasons, it requires its own recording, photographic reproduction, filming or video shooting, in short, its own transformation into images, documents, materials, objects to be achieved and preserved. Under this aspect the shift of the greatest theorist of theatrical performance, Richard Schechner, from a conception of scene as *actualizing*, implementation and presentification, to an idea of theatrical activity as *restoration*, recovering past behaviour, manipulation and transmission of a legacy, is significant. In short, it would seem that the more one emphasizes the instantaneity, immediacy and facticity of performance, the more one is driven to a conservative, regulative and witnessing attitude.

But witnessing what? If the boundary between scenic action and everydayness are not clearly traced, because on the one hand, current behaviours are understood as representations and, on the other, theatrical facts are modelled and blurred with behaviours and rituals of real life, the performative attitude goes beyond any extreme and permeates the entire existence not only of the professional actor but of any agent in whatever contest. However, if we are all *performers*, more or less able and capable, the exigency to provide a unique, singular, incomparable performance becomes even more incumbent and pressing upon us. Tradition provides two models of excellence, spiritual and physical, in which the aspirations of the performers can be channelled: holiness and athleticism, which from time immemorial have been the archetypes of supremacy and exceptionality. Hagiographic Orientalism and choreographic athleticism have permeated the experience of the theatrical avant-garde which has done nothing more than manifest tendencies and inclinations deeply rooted in the collective imagination. Martin Scorsese has depicted precisely these tendencies in his film *Cape Fear*, which tells the story of a man unjustly condemned to a long period of imprisonment, who undergoes a very tough spiritual and physical training that transforms him into a kind of superman, finally capable of getting even for all the wrongs he has suffered.

The superman, however, is still a man and not a thing. Even though a reification, a shift from the spirit to the sacred thing, and from the vital body to the body–thing, is already inherent in holiness, but even more in sacredness, and already in athleticism, but even more in sport, it is only with the entrance into a world in which there is no difference between the sacred and the profane, competitive sports and extreme para-sports activities, that this process reaches its fulfilment. Now the performance of a sentient thing is not the competitive performance of a subject with respect to others. The opposition between the saint and the mass of the damned, or between the winner and the crowd of losers, has a meaning only in a humanistic horizon. Whenever we move into the territory of the neutral and sentient thing, excellence acquires another meaning. It is the overcoming of oneself and one's own limits, not those of others. And the limits are two, the spirit and the body; in fact it is only one, the incarnate spirit, also said to be the living body.

Paradoxically, to accomplish this jump into the inorganic sentient world, one needs to be, perhaps, spiritually and physically not ahead of normality but a little behind. A handicap is necessary, a mental or a physical disadvantage, that can come from practising philosophy or the arts, or from disease or from a sensorial handicap, or both. The performance of the thing is not normal, but perverse. In the sexological sense, it is perverse because it derives excitement from inadequate stimulation, in fact, greatly inadequate, such as concepts, numbers, sounds, spaces, objects, writings, all things that normal people keep immersed in a functional–utilitarian boredom, or in an aesthetic–formal tedium.

To be sure, one has to wonder that philosophy and the arts are no longer organic parts of contemporary society, that they no longer constitute a necessary element of its self-representation, to the point of being similar to a handicap, a disadvantage. However, it is more than legitimate to ask whether the time has not come to do away with all those spiritual–vitalistic metaphors that have led us to consider society as a living organism. In fact, contemporary society has become inorganic, that is capable of being understood much more through the perverse effects of performances that take place in it than through the actions of projecting and programming subjects. The sexualization of philosophy and the arts is probably a perverse effect, that is an unforeseen and undesirable consequence provoked by the political irrelevance of these activities. But an even more perverse effect would be that through the sex appeal of the inorganic one would re-establish a live relation between them and society.

Notes

1. Walter Benjamin, 'Paris, Capital of the Nineteenth Centgury', *Reflections. Essays, Aphorisms, Autobiographical Writings*, trans. Edmund Jephcott (New York and London: Harcourt Brace Jovanovitch, 1978), p. 153.
2. René Descartes, *Meditationes de prima Philosophia/Meditations on First Philosophy*. A Bilingual Edition, trans. George Heffernan (Notre Dame and London: University of Notre Dame Press, 1990), Meditation II, 12.
3. Immanuel Kant, *Lectures on Ethics*, trans. Louis Infield (New York: Harper Torchbooks, Harper & Row, 1963).
4. Luigi Tansillo (1510–68), Lucanian writer of erotic lyrics [translator's note].
5. Karl Marx, *Capital*, I, i, 4.
6. Martin Heidegger, *Discourse on Thinking*, trans. John M. Anderson and E. Hans Freund (New York, Evanston, San Francisco, London: Harper & Row, Harper Colophon Books, 1966), p. 89.
7. G. W. F. Hegel, *The Phenomenology of Mind*, trans. J. B. Baille (New York and Evanston: Harper Torchbooks, Harper & Row, 1967), Pt. A, II, p. 164.
8. Ernst Bloch, 'Italy and Porosity', *Literary Essays*, trans A. Joron *et al.* (Stanford, CA: Stanford University Press, 1998), p. 455.
9. Edgar Allan Poe, 'For Annie', *Poems and Essays* (London: Dent, 1969).
10. G. W. F. Hegel, *The Encyclopedia of Philosophy in Outline and Critical Writings*, trans. Steven A. Taubeneck, ed. Ernst Behler (New York: Continuum, 1990) no. 140 note.
11. Martin Heidegger, 'The Origin of the Work of Art', *Poetry, Language, Thought*, trans. Albert Hofstadter (New York, Evanston, San Francisco, London: Harper & Row, 1971), p. 69.
12. Martin Heidegger, 'The Thing', *Poetry, Language, Thought*, p. 180. All further references are in the text.
13. Ludwig Wittgenstein, *Philosophical Investigations*, trans. G. E. M. Anscombe (New York: Macmillan, 1953), II, xi, p. 213. All further references are in the text.
14. Ludwig Wittgenstein, *Remarks on the Philosophy of Psychology*, vol. I, trans. G. E. M. Anscombe (Oxford: Basil Backwell, 1980), no. 167. [Anscombe's translation of this passage is: 'it is a matter of something's *coming into one's head*'. I have chosen to translate literally from Perniola's Italian, since the Italian translation of the Wittgenstein passage is important to the meaning that Perniola is trying to convey. Translator's note.]
15. Jacques Lacan, *Le Séminaire*. Livre XX Encore (1972–3) (Paris: Seuil, 1975).

Index of Names

ATHLONE CONTEMPORARY EUROPEAN THINKERS

Aesthetic Theory
Adorno
0 485 30069 9   HB

Composing for the Films
Adorno & Eisler
0 485 11454 2   HB
0 485 12017 7   PB

Freud and Nietzsche
Assoun
0 485 11483 6   HB

Criticism and Truth
Barthes
0 485 11321 X   PB

Sollers Writer
Barthes
0 485 11337 6   PB

On Nietzsche
Bataille
0 485 30068 0   HB

Nietzsche: The Body and Culture
Blondel
0 485 11391 0   HB

Death: An Essay on Finitude
Dastur
0 485 11487 9   HB

**Telling Time: Sketch of a
Phenomenological Chronology**
Dastur
0 485 11520 9   HB

Proust and Signs
Deleuze
0 485 12141 7   PB

Kant's Critical Philosophy
Deleuze
0 485 12101 8   PB

Difference and Repetition
Deleuze
0 485 11360 0   HB
0 485 12102 6   PB

The Fold: Leibniz and the Baroque
Deleuze
0 485 11421 6   HB
0 485 12087 9   HB

**Anti-Oedipus: Capitalism and
Schizophrenia**
Deleuze & Guattari
Preface by Michel Foucault
0 485 30018 4   PB

A Thousand Plateaus
Deleuze & Guattari
0 485 11335 X   HB
0 485 12058 5   PB

Cinema 1: The Movement-Image
Deleuze
0 485 12081 X   PB

Cinema 2: The Time-Image
Deleuze
0 485 11359 7   HB
0 485 12070 4   PB

Dialogues
Deleuze & Parnet
0 485 11333 3   HB

Foucault
Deleuze
0 485 12154 9   PB

Logic of Sense
Deleuze
0 485 30063 X   HB

Nietzsche and Philosophy
Deleuze
0 485 12053 4   PB

Dissemination
Derrida
0 485 12093 3   PB

Positions
Derrida
0 485 30000 1   HB
0 485 12055 0   PB

**The Memory of Thought:
On Heidegger and Adorno**
Duttman
0 485 11489 5   HB

**The Gift of Language: Memory
and Promise in Adorno, Benjamin,
Heidegger and Rosenzweig**
Duttman
0 485 11488 7   HB

Nietzsche's Philosophy
Fink
0 485 11484 4   HB

**Death and the Labyrinth: The
World of Raymond Roussel**
Foucault
0 485 11336 8   HB
0 485 12059 3   PB

Job: The Victim of his People
Girard
0 485 11304 X   HB

**Things Hidden Since the
Foundation of the World**
Girard
0 485 11307 4   HB

The Scapegoat
Girard
0 485 11306 6   HB

Violence and the Sacred
Girard
0 485 11341 4   PB

Deceit, Desire and the Novel
Girard
0 485 12067 4   PB

**To Double Business Bound:
Essays on Literature, Mimesis and
Anthropology**
Girard
0 485 11343 0   HB

Pleroma – Reading in Hegel
Hamacher
0 485 11457 7   HB

**Towards the Definition of
Philosophy**
Heidegger
0 485 11508 5   HB

The Nature of Truth
Heidegger
0 485 11509 3   HB

**On the Essence of Human
Freedom**
Heidegger
0 485 11516 6   HB

**Phenomenology of Intuition and
Expression**
Heidegger
0 485 11515 8   HB

Speech is Never Neuter
Irigaray
0 485 11452 9   HB
0 485 12089 5   PB

Democracy Between Two
Irigaray
0 485 11503 4   HB
0 485 12123 9   PB

To Be Two
0 485 11492 5   HB
0 485 12120 4   PB

The Forgetting of Air
Irigaray
0 485 11491 7   HB
0 485 12119 0   PB

Elemental Passions
Irigaray
0 485 11409 7   HB
0 485 12079 8   PB

**Thinking the Difference:
For a Peaceful Revolution**
Irigaray
0 485 11426 7   HB
0 485 12090 9   PB

An Ethics of Sexual Difference
Irigaray
0 485 30067 2   HB
0 485 30070 2   PB